Yearbook Adviser Survival Guide

The Yearbook Adviser Survival Guide

c. 2012 by Kari Molter, M. A.

All marketing and publishing rights guaranteed and reserved by the author.

Contact Information:
whywalk63@gmail.com

Please feel free to contact me with any questions or your thoughts about this book. I love to talk about yearbook!

Yearbook Adviser Survival Guide

Table of Contents

Introduction .... 4 - 6

Important Terminology .... 7 - 10

First Things First .... 11 - 14

Building a Staff .... 15 - 24

Staff Organization and Grading .... 25 - 42

Monthly Calendar of Tasks .... 41 - 50

Building a Classroom Environment .... 51 - 54

The Money Game .... 55 - 68

Digital Organization .... 69 - 72

Yearbook Distribution .... 753 - 74

Basic Training Teacher Guide .... 75 - 108

Basic Training Student Packet .... 109 - 140

Other Potentially Useful Stuff .... 141 - 147

Appendix 148

Yearbook Adviser Guide

INTRODUCTION

Twenty-five years ago, I was fresh out of college, desperate to never eat another package of macaroni and cheese or ramen noodles again. Out went the resumes and my hopes with them.

It came as a total surprise when the high school I graduated from contacted me for an interview. In the interview I was told that the position would involve teaching three courses: General Studies Ninth Grade English (no problem…), Theater (okay, I had experience working backstage and playing a wall in The Fall of the House of Usher my senior year), and Yearbook. I would have agreed to teach math if necessary (my weakest subject ever) …I wanted a job.

When they offered the job to me, I didn't hesitate. I also didn't know what I was getting myself into. English and Theater went fairly well.

That first year in yearbook class, however, was… interesting, to say the least. I had a fall delivery (thank goodness) 169 (or so) page book to produce with no idea how to do it. I was in a different classroom every hour. I had the principal's daughter on my staff. I had a classroom full of students who had expected the art teacher (a very fun but not so demanding guy) but got me, a somewhat neurotically organized taskmaster. I ended up kicking one student out of class toward the end of the year for nearly asphyxiating us when he took off his stinky tennis shoes one hot day and placed them on the open window ledge (okay, he had done some other things before that too).

I had absolutely no idea what to do. I knew we had to create a book… somehow… but I had no idea where to start. I do remember we had two typewriters and a couple of students who had been on the staff the previous year. I guess we had a camera somewhere, too.

At some point near the beginning of the year my yearbook sales representative showed up and introduced himself. He had a box of materials… what I later figured out to be three part layout sheets and forms we were to use to type out our copy. I was thrilled to see him and had a hundred questions. He gave me the box of materials, stayed for about a half hour, patted me on the top of my head (literally… he really patted me on top of my head)… and then he left, never to be seen again. Oh wait, he did give me these words of advice: "Don't worry sweetie… you'll figure it out and be just fine." I made a mental note to change yearbook companies as soon as possible and turned to the girl who would become my edior in chief. Between Jill and Heather and a few other hardworking kids, we put together a book.

Looking back today, I have no idea how we did it. The book would have never won any awards, but we got it done.

This is why I have wanted to put together a guide like this for a long time… so advisers can have a place to start when they are told that they will be the new yearbook adviser at their school. I know that I am always looking for ways to improve my classes so I also hope it might also be useful for an experienced adviser who is looking for a way to improve his or her class and publication.

What this book is…

► It is a practical guide for getting yearbook advisers organized. It puts together what I have learned over the last twenty-five years creating yearbooks… how to put a staff together, train them, make the classroom run efficiently, sell yearbooks, meet a budget, and create a publication that staff, students, and the community can be proud of. Although it may look complicated and overwhelming, I try to follow the "KISS" (Keep It Simple, Stupid) method as much as possible.

► It is my way of advising a yearbook… at the moment. I'm always changing things to make this process better for all involved… to create a better book that is a better value for the students… to include more kids… on and on and on. Use this publication as a guide… a place to begin developing your own way.

What this book is not…

► It is not intended to be a guide for creating a book intended to win immediate awards from a group like the Columbia Scholastic Press Association or any other group of that sort. Go to the websites mentioned in the appendix and get some of their publications for that. Implement a good organization such as I describe here, and you can end up with an award-winner if you want one. My personal opinion on the awards given out each year is that it can be great if that is your goal. It's a worthwhile goal. It's just not mine… at the moment. By the time our fall book arrives, most of my staff is gone. The real test for me is whether the students, staff, and community like the book.

► It is not the answer to <u>all</u> of your questions. I advise a 300 page yearbook that serves a suburban high school with approximately 1200 students in it, grades 9-12. Yearbook is a class… not an after school club. We are located on the fringes of an economically depressed city where many of my students' parents have lost their high-paying factory jobs in the automobile industry. We don't have a town… just a suburban area and a high school that is the center of our little community. This is the environment in which all of this was created. I think much of it can be "tweaked" to work in your school, however.

Notes:

IMPORTANT TERMINOLOGY

IMPORTANT TERMINOLOGY

Before I get into how to do this, you first need a vocabulary lesson. The following terms will come up again and again in this guide, and you will need to teach them to your students, so you might as well start now. More terms appear in the "Basic Training" section at the end of this publication.

Parts of a yearbook:

- Cover – this one is easy.

- Signature – 16 pages and Flat – 8 pages. A book is printed on a huge printing press where eight pages (one flat) at a time are printed on each side of a large sheet of paper. When both sides of the signature have been printed, then the large sheet is folded up into a 16 page booklet. Your yearbook consists of many of these booklets. If you want to really understand this, take a piece of 8 ½ by 11" paper. Fold it in half, then in half again, then in half for a third time. This will make a booklet about 3 ½ inches tall and 2 inches wide. If you look at the booklet you will find there are 16 pages in it. This is a small version of the signature you will use in a yearbook. If you look at the top of your book at the spine, you can see the booklets. This becomes important when planning out color in your book because you buy color by the flat (color pages go through the press one flat at a time, once for a black and white page and four times for a color page).

- Endsheets – the pages that hold the cover to the rest of the book. There are front and back endsheets.

- Spine – the part of the cover where the signature booklets are sewn together. When the book is standing up on a bookshelf with other books, you see its spine.

- Title page – the first page of the book after the front endsheets. It lists the theme, your school name, the year, and other information like that. It also introduces the theme.

- Colophon – the last page of the book. It gives publication information (staff names, publisher, sales representative's name, etc.)

Organizational Terms:

- Deadlines – The real dates pages are due to the publisher.

- Student Deadlines – The deadline dates you give to your students so you can actually meet the company deadlines.

- Theme – The idea that holds your book together.

- Ladder – A list of the content of each of the pages in the book. (An example appears in the appendix)

Layout Terms:
- Mugs / Mugshots – "school" pictures of each student

- DPS – Double Page Spread. Open up any book in front of you. You will see a left page and a right page. That's a DPS.

Notes:

FIRST THINGS FIRST

WHAT YOU NEED TO DO FIRST…

Maybe it's June and your principal enters your classroom with a guilty look on his face. He tells you that you will be advising the yearbook next year due to… budget cuts, teacher layoffs, retirements, and / or NCLB (no child left behind) requirements and you are "highly qualified" to do this.

Perhaps it's the end of the summer. You are a first year teacher like I was, desperate for a job and you would agree to anything… so you take a job that requires you to be the yearbook adviser. You believe your energy and enthusiasm will get you through.

Energy and enthusiasm is essential. It will, of course, help, but you need to get organized… and don't know where to start.

Well, start here.

Talk to someone in your school with experience.

If you can, grab the previous adviser or a student who has been in the class before and who will (hopefully) continue with you as adviser. If necessary, a department chairperson, curriculum coordinator, or principal might help. Ask a million questions…

- Who is the book's publishing company?

- Who is the sales representative? What is his or her telephone number?

- When do the books get delivered? Spring (before the students leave for the summer) or Fall?

- Is there a summer workshop put on by the publishing company that you could attend?

- What kind of class are the students expecting to see?

- Does the adviser have any materials you could use? Is there a curriculum?

- How do they sell the books?

- How are books distributed?

- Is there a copy of the most recent book that you could look over?

- Who are the returning students? Who will be the class leaders? Have any editors been chosen yet?

- Is there an application process for the class? Any prerequisites? What kind of kids will I be getting?

- Is there a school photographer? How do mug shots get taken? Sports pictures? (Our school, by the way, has a professional photographer who takes all of the sports individual and team photos. We also have them take some action shots for us… get that put in their contract if you can. It can be a life-saver later. They also come in for a day and take group photos of all of our clubs and organizations.)

- Does the class have cameras the students use?

- Does the class use computers? What kind of layout software? Adobe InDesign? On-line design?

- Where do things stand as far as budget? How much money does the staff have? Will another payment be due in the fall for the previous year's book? How much does it usually cost to produce the book?

- How many pages does the book typically have? Is it all color or all black and white? A combination? (If it is a combination understand that typically, color pages will have an earlier deadline than other pages.)

Contact your publisher's sales representative.

Summer is the slowest time of the year for him or her, so sacrifice some of your summer and meet with your representative. It is his or her job to help you! Schedule several days with this person, especially if you have missed the summer workshop.

- Get the questions above answered.

- Have your representative show you how to use the software you will be using. Preparing over the summer will make the school year run so much more smoothly. If I were a first year adviser with no software experience, I would probably use the on-line design system all publishers provide at this point. It is much easier than trying to learn Adobe In Design and Photo Shop. If you have a student or two who does know the programs, however, I think it is very useful for all students to learn them. They learn quickly, and the programs are used in the printing industry. They can leave your class with valuable real-world skills. Your students can teach you how to use them, too!

- Find out how much your yearbook will cost you. If you can find out how much the book cost the previous year, that would be helpful. Remember that your sales rep is there to help you, but he or she works for a profit-making company that is looking to make money. I have found that when a book is first put out for bid, many companies will come in with a very low price, then implement big increases in the years that follow or charge a huge amount for corrections. Be careful.

- Find out what your company deadlines will be. Yearbook companies often have promotions that will allow you to get things for "free" (like a custom cover or endsheets) if you submit a certain number of pages by a certain date. Get this information into your calendar.

- Have your sales representative help you set deadlines for your students. Never let your students know the real deadlines! Give yourself plenty of time, at least a month, in my experience, to get the pages to the company.

- Ask your sales rep if he or she knows of any experienced advisers in the area you could contact. This could be a life-saver for you. Most are more than willing to share. We remember what it was like trying to get this rolling our first year.

- Set a budget.

- Create a ladder diagram for your book.

- Possibly create student deadlines. I have my editors do this at the beginning of the year when I know exactly how many students will be in my class after all of the schedule changes happen.

- Make sure you can use the computer programs your students will be using.

- Have your representative help you with your basic training portion of the class. Begin with what you find in this book, if you like, then look at your publisher's educational offerings.

- <u>Don't try to do everything your first year. Do what you can. Get the book out. Learn. Have fun with your students. It takes several years to get good at teaching any class.</u>

BUILDING A STAFF

BUILDING A STAFF

Okay, crisis management completed. Let's start at the beginning. If you have the opportunity to do so, I recommend working hard at building yourself a strong staff. This may be something you won't be able to do until your second year, but whenever you get the opportunity, here's how to do it.

Some schools only let upperclassmen onto the yearbook staff. I disagree with this policy. I have many students who enter my class as sophomores who continue on all three years. It is essential to have veteran staffers to serve as leaders.

Our state has increased the graduation requirements for our students over the last five years, which has really hurt elective courses such as yearbook. I have been able to get my class approved for a "Fine Arts" credit, and this has helped many students fit the class into their schedule.

Institute an Application Process

That first year, I didn't have the opportunity to pick my staff. I was given a class of students who thought that the class would be one big party. This was a big hurdle to overcome. If that is what you are given, you can work with that for the first year. Get to know your kids and attach yourself to any kids who have been on the staff before. They will be your teachers.

For your second year, go to your administration and make a case for allowing you to institute an application process. There are plenty of reasons why you should have the power to choose your staff. Here are just a few:

- This book is the one and only record of this school year.
- This class is a business. The classroom will not look like a typical classroom with students all doing the same thing. Therefore responsible students are very important for the book's success. I need to know that everyone will be doing his or her job.
- Students may need to be out of the classroom taking pictures and interviewing students and teachers during class time… therefore this will be a temptation for irresponsible students to wander.
- Students, parents, and community members all read this book. It needs to be something that will be a positive public relations tool. If the classroom is filled with students who are not dedicated to the project the quality of the product will suffer.

I currently use a written application, with interviews as a back-up. Our newspaper adviser interviews his applicants along with an application. I never seem to have the time to interview everyone.

The kind of students I look for are responsible kids. They don't have to be the top kids in the school… just hard workers who won't wander the hallways and who are excited about working on the yearbook.

I like the application that follows at the end of this chapter because it is simple. The kids evaluate themselves, then I get to compare their self-evaluation to their teachers' opinions. It is important that the teachers return their recommendation forms to me or my school mailbox, not the students. Any teacher forms that are given to me by the students are automatically suspect. I also go to our on-line student maintenance system and look at the students' grades and teacher comments for my applicants. I'm looking for comments like "courteous and cooperative" and "makes a good effort". I can check attendance there, too.

Announcements

Do students listen to the announcements at your school? It is a hit and miss thing at my school, but I do run an announcement that usually goes something like the one below. It is pretty simple:

> Announcement:
> Apply to be on next year's yearbook staff! The ECHO is looking for responsible, enthusiastic staff members to preserve next year's memories. Pick up an application from your counselor or outside room 106. Applications are due to Mrs. Molter by THIS FRIDAY, February 15 and schedules will be signed on Monday, February 18.

Classroom Visits

I have had very good luck visiting the honors English classrooms to recruit kids, but I recruit from all grade levels and abilities. I try to include special needs students whenever I can, modifying their work to included fewer deadlines. This is a good experience for the other students and gives the special needs students the chance to be mainstreamed and feel less isolated. Art classes are another good place to recruit, except it needs to be made clear to the kids that this is not an art class or an hour to "scrapbook"; they will write, too! You will need younger kids to stay in the class for multiple years and become your editors, so don't let the class be dominated by seniors.

Mine Your Own Classroom

When I taught Freshman English, I recruited kids from my classroom. I also teach Creative Writing and recruit kids from there as well. Kids are really flattered when you tell them that they should be on your staff. You have experience with them so you know what you are getting.

Ask for Help from your Colleagues

Sending an e-mail to the Language Arts Department (or the entire High School staff) has also proven useful in the past. I ask them to nominate students for the staff and I then send them an invitation to apply with an application attached.

Posters

I do put up posters around the school. This probably brings in a few kids. Make sure the poster advertises where applications can be picked up, where to turn them in, and the deadline date.

Get Your Current Staffers to recommend their Friends

Good kids have good friends. Send them an application. This probably brings in most of my staff.

THINKING ABOUT JOINING THE YEARBOOK STAFF? READ THIS!

The yearbook staff produces Kearsley High School's award-winning 300- page yearbook, the <u>Echo</u>. You probably already know that, but there are some things about the class you probably don't know.

If you were to look into the yearbook staff room, what might you see? The production of this book does not take place in a typical high school classroom atmosphere. First of all, you won't find many students in the classroom. You would see some students being helped by the editors of the book (students who have been in the class for more than one year), and other editors checking pages before we send them to the plant. Some students are always around the photo computer where we download, edit, and choose all the digital images we use in the book. Most students are out interviewing people, taking pictures, or working on their pages (doing layouts and writing copy) in the computer lab. Some days you will see hot pizza, a submarine sandwich, or even homemade cheesecake and chocolate peanut-butter ice-cream pie as the staff celebrates a completed deadline.

As a staffer, you will be responsible for all aspects of your pages. The first quarter of the class is spend in what we call "basic training" where you will learn how to write journalistically, create layouts, and use our computer program (Adobe In Design) among other things. We will also all work together selling advertisements to keep the price of the book low and to give YOU the chance to earn a free yearbook. After you are trained, creating your pages will be your focus for the rest of the year. You will decide what you need to do in class each day to complete your pages and meet your deadlines. Your grade will be based on meeting your deadlines.

So if you are a responsible person who likes long-term projects, this is the class for you! You don't have to be the world's greatest writer, just someone who is willing to learn and work hard… and have some fun, too!

Complete this application, get three teachers to fill out recommendation forms, and return all of this to Mrs. Molter **by February 15**. The staff list will be posted outside room 106 and schedules will be signed **on February 18**.

Don't forget that your application and letters are due to Mrs. Molter by February 15th!

YEARBOOK STAFF APPLICATION

Name _____ **Grade (next year)** _____

Please answer the following questions completely!
Don't forget to give this application and your three letters of recommendation to Mrs. Molter in room 106 (or you could put it in her mailbox in the main office) by February 23rd!

1. I would be a great yearbook staff member because…

2. Evaluate yourself in the following areas:

	Excellent	Very Good	Not Bad	I need to work on this.
I am a responsible person.	5	4	3	2	1
I like to work with other students on projects.	5	4	3	2	1
I sometimes go above and beyond an assignment.	5	4	3	2	1
I am a hard worker.	5	4	3	2	1
It is important to me that I produce quality work.	5	4	3	2	1
I'm willing to take direction from others.	5	4	3	2	1
I don't get frustrated when having to re-do work to make it perfect.	5	4	3	2	1
My ability to meet deadlines…	5	4	3	2	1
My overall attitude is…	5	4	3	2	1
Writing Skills are…	5	4	3	2	1
My attendance is…	5	4	3	2	1

3. My schedule this year:

Hour	Class	Teacher	First Sem. Grade
1	_____	_____	_____
2	_____	_____	_____
3	_____	_____	_____
4	_____	_____	_____
5	_____	_____	_____
6	_____	_____	_____

4. I have asked the following teachers to fill out a recommendation form for me:

_____
_____
_____

5. Looking at last year's yearbook, what do you like about it? What would you like to see changed?

6. I am interested in attending the yearbook workshop in June. ___ yes ___ no (explain)

I have read the class description on the front page of this application and understand the responsibilities involved in being a member of the yearbook staff.

Student Signaure _____

Parent Signature _____

Teacher Recommendation Form
Kearsley High School Yearbook Staff

Student: Fill in the information in this box and deliver to a teacher who knows you well. YOU MUST HAVE THREE RECOMMENDATIONS TOTAL. <u>Teachers</u> will return this form to Mrs. Molter.

Student Name: _____ Grade (next year): 10 11 12

Dear Staff Member,

The student above has applied for the Yearbook Staff. Please complete this form and return it to my mailbox by February 23rd.

Thank-you.

Kari Molter

	Excellent		Questionable		Poor	N/A
Responsibility level	5	4	3	2	1	N/A
Ability to work well with others.	5	4	3	2	1	N/A
Initiative	5	4	3	2	1	N/A
Work Ethic	5	4	3	2	1	N/A
Concerned with producing quality work.	5	4	3	2	1	N/A
Willing to take direction.	5	4	3	2	1	N/A
Does not get frustrated when having to re-do work to make it perfect.	5	4	3	2	1	N/A
Ability to meet deadlines	5	4	3	2	1	N/A
Overall Attitude	5	4	3	2	1	N/A
Writing Skills	5	4	3	2	1	N/A
Attendance	5	4	3	2	1	N/A
Overall recommendation	**5**	**4**	**3**	**2**	**1**	**N/A**

Comments:

Teacher Signature _____

Yearbook Adviser Survival Guide

YEARBOOK STAFF VETERAN INTEREST SURVEY

Name _____ Grade (Next Year) _____

Telephone Number _____

1. I am interested in attending the yearbook workshop on June 28-29. The $220 payment is due no later than next Wednesday, June 6.

    ____yes, I will attend   ____ maybe, I can let you know <u>tomorrow</u>

    ____no, I cannot attend

Comments/Concerns:

2. I am interested in selling and distributing yearbooks at registration in August. Working a two-hour shift will exempt me from having to distribute yearbooks at homecoming.

    ____yes   ____no

Comments/Concerns:

3. I am interested in the following leadership positions:

    ____ Chief Editor
    ____ Photo Editor
    ____ Team Leader
    ____ Social Director

Comments/Concerns:

4. If I could change one thing about our yearbook it would be…

Notes:

STAFF ORGANIZATION and GRADING

Staff Organization and Grading

So you have picked your staff or your staff has been picked for you. How do you get organized?

I have used a variety of organizations over the years, and continually tweak this depending on the number of returning students and the strengths of those students. For me, I have found that staff organization and grading students goes hand in hand. I therefore organize my staff so that each student knows his or her role and how each grade will be determined.

I'll describe three different classroom organizations that I have used in the past. The final one is what I use now.

Organization by Jobs

In this type of organization, there is one editor in chief in charge of the overall product and students either write copy, design layouts, take pictures, or sell advertising. Although students might get to pick the job they will do according to their interests (creating layouts, writing copy, taking pictures, selling advertisements), they basically do the same thing all year long.

This is my least favorite type of classroom organization. I found it hard to grade and make sure all of the pages got done on time. It seemed that everyone was always blaming someone else. There are many variations to this type of organization I would imagine, like having a student (probably an editor) in charge of getting all of the elements for a page or section together. A section editor could be in charge of those pages and make sure that everyone working on a page completes their work on time.

One advantage to this organization includes having one person in charge of every page in a particular section so consistency is easier to achieve. I did not like the fact that this organization did not give students experience in all areas of creating a publication, however.

The jobs are:

- Editor in Chief
- Photography Editor
- Photographers
- Advertising Editor
- Names Editor
- Copy Writers
- Layout Designers

These are the different sections of a yearbook... a section editor could be assigned for each or one student could also be a section leader for several sections.
- Student Life
- Sports
- Faculty
- Academics
- Mugshots (student school pictures)
- Senior section
- Clubs and Organizations

Section Leader Organization

I used this organization for many years until we decided to start submitting our book using the PDF format through the internet which caused us to change again.

In this organization, each student is responsible for a number of pages in the yearbook... all elements of each page. This way, students gain experience in nearly all aspects of producing a publication. They are also responsible for selling about $300 worth of ads.

My editors and I set up the ladder (a list of the topic on each double page spread, there is an example later in this publication) then break that down into individual deadlines, taking into consideration school events, sports seasons, and so on.

The jobs are:
- Editor in Chief (1 person)
- Copy Editor
- Advertising Editor
- Photo Editor
- Section Editors
  - Student Life
  - Sports
  - Faculty
  - Academics
  - Mugs
  - Seniors
  - Clubs and Organizations
- Newbie / Rookie Staffers
- Warden (the class enforcer who would handle passes and make sure all stayed on task)

My year would go this way: I would usually have my editors chosen by the end of the previous year so that they can gather ideas for their sections over the summer.

In the fall, the editors would prepare section templates and get deadlines organized for the first few weeks when I would be training the rookie staffers. By the time the rookies learned about the basics of yearbook journalism, how to create layouts, how to write copy, how to take pictures, and how to use the computer program the templates for each section would be done. My editor in chief would approve them then I would approve them. We would place the section templates on blank InDesign pages on our network or into our company's Online Design program, then the kids would go to work. They would have a deadline about once a month. More details on how pages get checked and grades get assigned later.

Team Leader Organization

This is the organization that I currently prefer. It evolved from the Section Organization above.

In this organization, each student is responsible for a number of pages in the yearbook just like the previous method... all elements of each page. This way, students gain experience in nearly all aspects of producing a publication.

My editors and I decided to set up the ladder in a slightly different way since the 2006-7 school year... we no longer have sections of the book like Student Life and Sports. Instead, we have organized our book according to the seasons. We have (obviously) four sections of the book... Fall, Winter, Spring, and Summer. In the fall we included events like homecoming, fall sports, and mug shots for freshmen. We decided to do this because we need to submit pages in flats in order to get a price break from our publisher and this made things easier for us overall. We break the ladder down into individual deadlines, taking into consideration school events, sports seasons, and so on. We also decided to put mug shots on all pages of the book... one year across the top of each page and in 2007-8 down the sides of the pages. This allowed us to have individual pages for each junior varsity and freshman sport instead of combining them on one page. After those two years we returned to dedicated pages for mug shots.

The jobs in detail are:

Submissions Editor (1 person)
- Ladder Creation
- Deadline Organization
- Final Page Check
- Submit Completed Pages
- Check and Resubmit Proofs
- The Submission Editor's grade will be determined through periodic evaluations by the adviser.

Chief Editor (1 person)
- Communicate with team leaders to meet deadlines / answer concerns
- Check pages (all elements) before submissions editor
- The Chief Editor's grade will be determined by an average of the team leader's grades, a conference with the adviser, and an evaluation by the rest of the staff.

Team Leaders (I used five in 2007-8)
- Lead up to five staff members as they prepare their pages.
- It is the team leader's responsibility to make sure that the staffers he or she is working with produce accurate, creative pages on time by helping staffers stay on task.
- Keep track of the whereabouts of their team members by monitoring the pass system.
- Be in charge of one section of the book (ie. sports pages, mugs, staff, seniors, etc.)

- Create template for their assigned section
- The Team Leader's grade is determined by averaging the deadline, creativity, and accuracy grades of each of their team members as well as evaluations each deadline from their team members.

Business Editor (1 person)
- Set the budget
- Organize Advertising Sales Day (Ad Areas, etc)
- Collect business advertisements and parent ads
- Organize and distribute ads to students assigned ads pages
- Bill advertisers
- Keep accurate records
- The Business Editor's grade will be determined through periodic evaluations by the adviser.

Photo Editor (1 person)
- Check out Cameras
- Download Cameras
- Monitor Batteries
- Make sure pictures are used only once… move them to student folders
- Organize / Coordinate with school photographer
- The Photo Editor's grade will be determined through periodic evaluations by the adviser.

Names Editor (1 person… new for 2009… I did not have one in 2008)
- Collect the name sheets collected at registration.
- Compare to the list to the list from the office
- Beginning with the previous year's file, delete last year's seniors and add all new students, including the freshmen. (We type all the names using upper and lower case letters since our school's list is in all caps.)
- Copy and distribute the names list to the staff.
- The Names Editor's grade will be determined through periodic evaluations by the adviser and by averaging the accuracy grade of each staffer.

Social Director (1 person)
- Team building activities
- Deadline parties (collect money, order pizza)
- Motivate students to get their deadlines in on time using positive reinforcement.

Staffers
- I usually have about 20 of these… some rookies, some returning staff members who do not want to be editors, some editors who are not serving as team leaders for a deadline or other editors who are completing a deadline
- Complete all elements of one Double Page Spread (DPS) per deadline
    o Interview appropriate people
    o Attend events related to their page (club meetings, sporting events, etc)
    o Take all pictures for their page
    o Create layout
    o Write all copy: headline, subhead, captions, body copy, scoreboard

Grading

I am fairly brutal about grading. I want to keep it simple, so here is what I do:

- right away at the beginning of the year, students pick their deadlines. The deadline date is written in stone, with very few exceptions. We have had our fall play, for example, turn into a winter play before, so that deadline had to change.
- Each deadline has three grades associated with it...
    - 100 points: meeting the deadline. If the page is accepted one week before the deadline, they get free food at the next party (we celebrate each time a deadline is met). If they get done at least one day early they get exam exemption for that deadline. If they get exam exemption on all of their deadlines each semester, they earn an automatic "A" on their exam. This is a huge motivation for them.
    - 100 points: creativity. I want a creative, appealing layout as well as interesting body copy and captions.
    - 100 points: accuracy. This means that every name is spelled and indexed correctly, and other information (ie. about sports seasons for example, is accurate).

That's it for staffers who are working a deadline. The students have a check sheet for each deadline. They do a self-check, have their team leader check it, have the copy editor (s) check it, then turn it in to me.

I look at it, and send it back with corrections. The grade they earn at this point for accuracy sticks. Every name that does not match the names list is -10. Every inaccuracy is -10. it's pretty high stakes. The number one complaint I get is over misspelled names.

If they get their corrections back to me within three days, they will earn their exemption.

Editors are a different story. Their grades are determined according to the criteria in their job descriptions mentioned earlier in this manual.

When I check a student's page, I usually have lots of pages to check, so I take a half sheet (below) and give the kids feedback in a written manner if I can't talk to them in person.

After my grade report, you will find a copy of one of my deadline sheets for last year. This form stays in a notebook on my desk and really helps keep me organized. I started using this form when we submitted our pages using the PDF format. The last two years, we have used our publisher's Online program. The program is very easy to use, and helps me keep track of proofed and submitted pages but I found myself still using the form because it helped me to know which pages were ready to be proofed and which were fixed, something the online program can't tell me. Books submitted over the internet, (the PDF method) should find a form like this very helpful. It should include the date the page was completed, the students' grades, the date the PDF was completed, the date the PDF was submitted, then the date the page was proofed as well as the date the page is finally submitted. This form helps to make sure a page isn't missed and again, makes sure everything gets in on time. I have reformatted the page to be a portrait orientation, but the sheets I use are landscape so there is room to write in the correct dates.

Grade Report
Deadline _____

Page Numbers _____   Staffer _____

Deadline: _____ of 100
Comments:

Creativity: _____ of 100
Comments:

Accuracy: _____ of 100
Comments:

Yearbook Adviser Survival Guide

DEADLINE #1

		Subject	Page #'s	Staffer	Due Date	Date Completed	Grade Deadline	Grade Creativity	Grade Accuracy	Date Proof Printed	Date Proof Fixed	Date Submitted
	1	Title/Colophon	1 / 288	Kylie	Dec 3							
	2	Opening	2-3	Katie	Dec 3							
	3	New Stuff	4-5	Brittany	Dec 3							
	4	Fall Div	6-7	Kelsey	Dec 3							
	5	Spirit Week	8-9	Jessica	Dec 3							
	6	Frs. Spirit week	10-11	Krista	Dec 3							
	7	Soph. Spirit Wk	12-13	Alyssa	Dec 3							
	8	Jr. Spirit Week	14-15	Kirsten	Dec 3							
	9	Sr. Spirit Week	16-17	Sam	Dec 3							
	10	Powder puff court	18-19	Terra	Dec 3							
	11	Powder puff game	20-21	Rachel	Dec 3							
	12	Homecoming Parade	22-23	Katie F	Dec 3							
	13	Homecoming Court	24-25	Trina	Dec 3							
	14	Homecoming Game	26-27	Josh	Dec 3							
	15	Homecoming Dance	28-29	Miranda	Dec 3							
	16	Marching Band	30-31	Ally	Dec 3							
	17	Open	32-33	Megan	Dec 3							
	18	Open	34-35	Sam G	Dec 3							
	19	Open	36-37	Cecily	Dec 3							
	20	Open	38-39	Paige	Dec 3							
	21	Lip Sync	40-41	Nicole	Dec 3							
	22	Freshmen Impressions	42-43	Sadie	Dec 3							
	23	Open	44-45	Diane	Dec 3							
	24	Girls JV golf	46-47	Mary	Dec 3							
	25	Girls Varsity Golf	48-49	Devan	Dec 3							
Template On Page File												

Editors

As noted in the job descriptions, I grade my editors through one-on-one conferences throughout the deadline. I also have my staffers fill out an evaluation form for each deadline evaluating their editors and I use these (with no specific student names mentioned) during my conference at the end of each deadline.

The editors also complete two to three spreads each year, and they are graded just like any regular staffer is graded. They become team members underneath a team leader in addition to their duties as editors. In that case, they end up having grades for their editorial work and grades for their DPS.

Ladder Diagram Example

xxxxxxxxxx	1	Title Page
2 Opening / Theme (pages 2-3 ... all topics carry across the DPS)	3	
4 Fall Division	5	
6 Student Life: Registration	7	
8 Student Life: First Days of School	9	
10 Student Life: Open	11	
12 Student Life: Open	13	
14 Student Life: Homecoming Parade	15	
16 Student Life: Homecoming Court	17	
18 Student Life: Homecoming Pep Assembly	19	
20 Freshmen Mugs	21	
22 Freshmen Mugs	23	
24 Freshmen Mugs	25	
26 Varsity Football	27	
28 JV / Freshman Football	29	
30	31	
32	33	
34	35	
36	37	
38	39	
40	41	
42	43	
44	45	
46	47	
48	49	
50	51	
52	53	
54	55	
56	57	
58	59	
60	61	
62	63	
64	65	
66	67	
68	69	
70	71	
72	73	
74 Index	75	
76 Index	77	
78 Closing	79	
80 Colophon		

Yearbook Staff Organization 2007-2008

Submissions Editor (Valerie)
General Duties:
- Ladder / General Organization
- Final page check
- Prepare final pages for submission
- Check and resubmit proofs

Chief Editor (Jade)
General Duties:
- Communicate with team leaders to meet deadlines / answer concerns
- Check pages (all elements) before Submissions editor

Business Editor (Casey)
General Duties:
- Set the budget
- Organize advertising sales day
- Collect business advertisements and parent ads
- Bill advertisers
- Keep accurate records

Photo Editor (Kristyn)
General Duties:
- Check out Cameras
- Download Cameras
- Monitor Batteries
- Make sure pics are used once / move pics to student folders
- Organize/Coordinate with Alternative Photographics

Team Leader	Team Leader	Team Leader	Team Leader	Team Leader
Rachel	Jenny	Samantha	Alannah	Alisha
Staffer	Staffer	Staffer	Staffer	Staffer
Staffer	Staffer	Staffer	Staffer	Staffer
Staffer	Staffer	Staffer	Staffer	Staffer
Staffer	Staffer	Staffer	Staffer	Staffer
Staffer	Staffer	Staffer	Staffer	Staffer

Team Leaders will lead up to five other staff members as they prepare their pages. It is the team leader's responsibility to make sure that the staffers he or she is working with produce accurate, creative pages on time by helping staffers stay on task and giving creative suggestions. Team leaders will also check the names, index, copy, pictures, and layout for each member of his or her team. The team leader's grade will be determined by averaging the deadline, creativity, and accuracy grades of each of their team members.

Staffers will be responsible for producing accurate, creative pages on time.

The Social Director will organize deadline parties, lead team-building activities, and work to keep up staff morale. This job could possibly be combined with one of the other editorial positions above.

Yearbook Adviser Survival Guide

Layout Approval Form - Staffer

Staffer _____ Page Numbers: _____-_____

Deadline: _____ Date Due: _____

STAFFER please initial each item when completed. Giving false information will affect your grade negatively.

I have carefully completed my page by accomplishing the following:

____ LAYOUT: My layout follows the instructions on the template for my section.

____ FONTS: Body Copy and byline is 10 pt. _____, Captions are 8 pt _____, Headlines are any other AWPC font that is appropriate.

____ BODY COPY: I have written body copy with an interesting lead, quote-transition format, and genuine quotations. No "YOU" except in quotes and perhaps in an interesting lead. Copy contains a lead, and at least 8 quotes and transitions.

____ CAPTIONS: I have written captions that name every person accurately with first and last names. Every first sentence is in present tense telling what is going on and every second sentence is in past tense telling more than the obvious. Second sentences are not filler, they give more interesting information.

____ HEADLINE:: Centered above body copy or in another location approved by your team leader., appropriate point size.

____ BYLINE: Located on the first line of copy, formatted properly (by Joe Yearbook)

____ JUSTIFICATION: All copy is justified (even on both sides of the column).

____ COLOR: Only Formula Colors are used, within a shade family / complimentary colors… not distratcting, copy is readable if a color is behind it…

____ NAMES/ INDEXING: Every name in my captions is spelled and indexed (CTRL-SHIFT-F8) correctly.

____ I have checked to see that every name in a caption is in the index. I have followed this process: go to window>index then print the index (click on the arrow on the right of the box and click on generate index. Place the text somewhere on the pasteboard, highlight with the "T" tool and copy, paste into a word document using multiple columns to save paper, print, then delete the index information in InDesign).

____ I have checked that every name is spelled correctly by checking my printout with the names list and making corrections in InDesign then printing a new index in Word.

____ No yearbook staffers are pictured unless he or she is involved in that group or club (ie. band, SADD, etc.)

____ PHOTOS: My pictures are interesting, clear, and show faces. They are action shots, not posed shots. All links are valid.

I certify that all of the above information is true and I have not fabricated any portion of my work. In my page folder is my reporters notebook pages for all quotes, for a sports page, a printout from the website from today, and an index printed today.

▶ Signature: _____   Date _____

Yearbook Adviser Survival Guide

Layout Approval Form - Editors

Staffer _____ Page Numbers: _____
Deadline: _____ Date Due: _____

TEAM LEADER: please initial each item when completed. Giving false information will affect your grade negatively.

I have carefully checked this page for the following:

____ LAYOUT: This layout follows the instructions on the template for my section.

____ FONTS: Body Copy and byline is 10 pt. _____, Captions are 8 pt _____, Headlines are any other AWPC font that is appropriate.

____ BODY COPY: This copy has an interesting lead, quote-transition format, and genuine quotations. No "YOU" except in quotes and perhaps in an interesting lead. Copy contains a lead, and at least 8 quotes and transitions.

____ CAPTIONS: This copy has captions that name every person accurately with first and last names. Every first sentence is in present tense telling what is going on and every second sentence is in past tense telling more than the obvious. Second sentences are not filler, they give more interesting information.

____ HEADLINE: Centered above body copy, appropriate point size.

____ BYLINE: Located on the first line of copy, formatted properly (by Joe Yearbook)

____ JUSTIFICATION: All copy is justified (even on both sides of the column).

____ COLOR: Only Formula Colors are used, within a shade family family / complimentary colors… not distratcting, copy is readable if a color is behind it.

____ NAMES/INDEX: I have personally checked every name on the most recent index printout to the names list and they are all correct. Every name in a caption is indexed. (Check that every name is indexed on the DPS, then check the spelling of every name. Make sure that corrections are made in InDesign.)

____ PHOTOS: The pictures are interesting, clear, and show faces. They are action shots, not posed shots. All links are valid.

I certify that this page is correct and complete.

▶ Team Leader Signature: _____ Date _____

▶ Chief Editor Signature: _____ Date _____

▶ Adviser Signature: _____ Date _____

Grades (to be determined by adviser):

_____ **(100) Deadline is met (early=110, on time =100, each class day thereafter =-10points per day). After 5 days the staffer will earn a "0" and the team leader has one week to finish the deadline and turn the team leader's grade for that deadline to a D- (60 points).**

_____ **(100) Accuracy (names/index/facts) Every name error (misspelling on page, misspelling on index, or name left off page) will subtract 10 points from this score.**

_____ **(100) Creativity (body copy and captions are interesting, layout is creative)**

Yearbook Adviser Survival Guide

"Evaluate Your Editors"

Name _____ Deadline 1 2 3 4 5 6

Your Team Leader _____

Grade your Team Leader in the following capacities, please...

Helpfulness:	A	B	C	D	E	NA
Knowledge of InDesign:	A	B	C	D	E	NA
Attitude:	A	B	C	D	E	NA
Availability (is she around when you need her?):	A	B	C	D	E	NA
Respectfulness:	A	B	C	D	E	NA

OVERALL: _____

Comments (what should she do to improve / what should she keep doing?):

Grade Jade (Chief Editor) in the following capacities, please...

Helpfulness:	A	B	C	D	E	NA
Knowledge of InDesign:	A	B	C	D	E	NA
Attitude:	A	B	C	D	E	NA
Availability: (is she around when you need her?):	A	B	C	D	E	NA
Respectfulness:	A	B	C	D	E	NA

OVERALL: _____

Comments (what should she do to improve / what should she keep doing?):

Grade Kristyn (Photo Editor) in the following capacities, please...

Helpfulness:	A	B	C	D	E	NA
Attitude:	A	B	C	D	E	NA
Availability (is she around when you need her?):	A	B	C	D	E	NA
Respectfulness:	A	B	C	D	E	NA

OVERALL: _____

Comments (what should she do to improve / what should she keep doing?):

Grade Casey (Advertising Editor) in the following capacities, please...

Helpfulness:	A	B	C	D	E	NA
Attitude:	A	B	C	D	E	NA
Availability (is she around when you need her?):	A	B	C	D	E	NA
Respectfulness:	A	B	C	D	E	NA

OVERALL: _____

Comments (what should she do to improve / what should she keep doing?):

Notes:

MONTHLY TASK CALENDAR

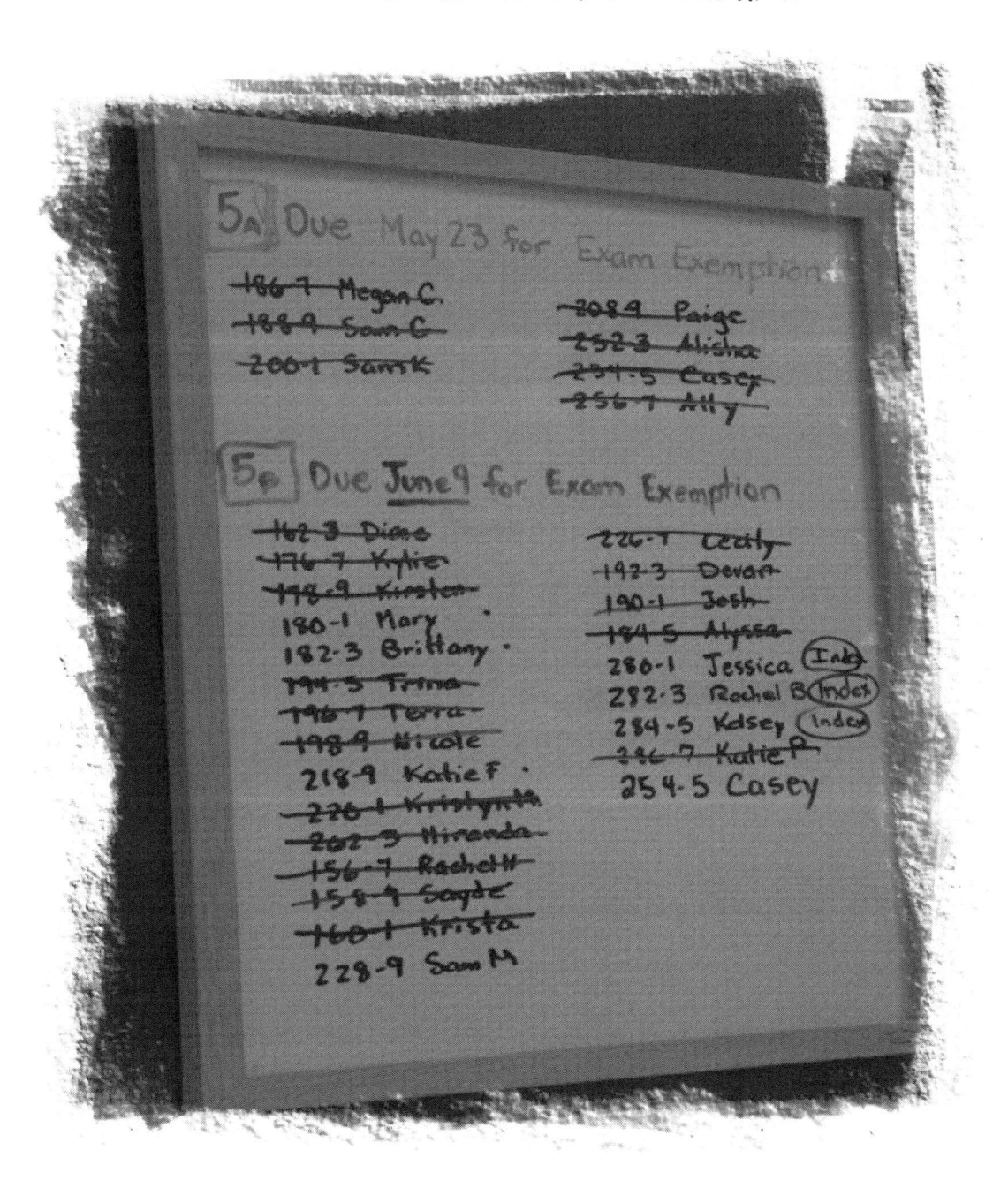

Monthly Task Calendar
(Fall Delivery Book)

I strongly believe that a fall book is the way to go. Luckily, this decision was made for me twenty-five years ago so I did not have to implement a change from a spring delivery myself. I could simply relate to the community that my principal made the decision for me.

Here is why I believe it is worthwhile to produce a fall delivery book:
- A fall delivery book will allow your staff to cover the entire school year. My last deadline is in mid to late June. If we had a spring delivery book, we would have to be done in April. In my book we cover all senior activities, spring sports, and end of year events. A spring delivery book cannot do that.
- The reason most people cite for having a spring delivery book is that they want their friends to sign it. You can provide pages for this purpose that will stick in the book provided by your publisher. Our graduation announcement company also sells such a book. It really is no big deal.
- What about the seniors? How will they get their books? We used to set up a booth at homecoming and deliver books there. It brings seniors back to the school so those books can be signed and lifts school spirit as well to see alumni come back for the big game. We also offer to mail the books to students for a $10 fee. We get to make a few bucks there, too.
- Now, we receive our books early enough that we distribute books at fall registration. Seniors or their parents come back to get them as many have younger siblings registering at that time. We call anyone who has not collected their book once school starts, and set up a couple of days after school for alumni to come get them. After that, people trickle in, coming in after or before school to get them throughout the year. We distribute about 80% of our books at registration.

If you have a spring delivery book, this schedule can easily be adjusted. Sit down with your sales representative and make your own calendar. Nonetheless, the same jobs need to be completed.

MAY / JUNE (previous school year)
For the publication you are finishing up...
- finish the yearbook for that year
- complete the proofing process
- organize the name plates (we tape them to the yearbook order forms. By the way, we much prefer the stick-on name plates to the names printed on the yearbooks themselves because a name plate with a mistake on it is easy to fix, where a book with a misspelled name is no good to anyone. We also appreciate not having to organize the books with names on them for distribution. Check out Seniors (use Senior Check-Out sheet)
- Check out Underclassmen (use underclassmen check-out sheet)

For next year's book...
- create yearbook application

- recruit and choose staff
- choose editors for the next year… consult current editors on staff
- Visit all junior English classrooms with the senior picture flyer. I do this personally so I can tell parents later that everyone received a flyer with our photo specifications and deadline.
- Send senior picture specifications to photography studios.
- attend your publisher's summer workshop
    - decide on the book's theme
    - create the cover, endsheets, division pages
    - create folio tab artwork (by the page number)
- plan budget
- set book prices
- create / order yearbook order forms and get them to the printer.
- organize returning students to work yearbook delivery if it is to take place at registration via a letter to next year's staff about the workshop and working registration.
- organize students to sell yearbooks at registration

JULY
- Don't think about yearbook!!!

AUGUST
Early - Mid August
- Make sure the office has the yearbook sales flyer to include in the summer registration packet. (If your school doesn't have summer registration days, recommend it to your administration. It sure is nice for us. Students have their school pictures taken, pay for parking permits, pick up their schedules, pay into their lunch accounts, pick-up their yearbook and purchase a yearbook for the current year. It avoids lots of classroom interruptions later and is awfully convenient for the yearbook adviser!)
- Make sure the office has the "how do you want your name spelled in the yearbook" flyer to include in the summer registration packet.
- Take delivery of the book!
- organize book delivery / call or text to remind students who will be working

Late August
- deliver yearbooks at registration
- sell yearbooks at registration

SEPTEMBER
- school starts
- mail yearbooks to those who paid for this service
- meet with sales representative to set deadlines and finalize budget
- evaluate the new book… what do we need to improve in this year's book?
- Team Building Activities
- Return book overruns for credit off the final bill if you think they won't sell.
- Editors

- o create page templates and check sheets
- o finalize ladder (We have an all-color book but if you don't, remember to organize your color by flats and place them in an early deadline.)
- o create deadlines (Make sure the deadlines you create for your students will fulfill the deadlines from your publisher... and don't let your kids know that these are not the actual deadlines from your publisher.)
- o choose fonts for body copy and captions
- o Business editor plans and begins ad sales and other fund-raisers
- o pay final invoice to the publisher
- Rookie Staffers
  - o Basic Training
  - o staffers choose deadlines (I have the editors conduct this by random draw... everyone writes their name on a card and it goes into a hat. First name chosen gets first choice each deadline. This usually ends up taking two class periods)

OCTOBER
- continue ad sales
- deliver yearbooks to graduates at homecoming and / or call them for pick-up
- plan November yearbook sales (we sell most of our books at registration before school even starts, but do mail home one flyer for the November "Final" sale).
- Mail flyer to senior parents for senior advertisements.
- Begin page production process
  - o Students begin their production jobs described earlier and start to work on deadlines.

NOVEMBER
- Schedule and execute group picture day (we use our auditorium and have a photographer come in and take photographs of all of the school groups... choirs, bands, and other clubs). The photographer who takes our sports pictures does this for us for free. The schedule we used last year can be found later in this chapter).
- Wrap-up advertising sales early this month.
- Production

DECEMBER, JANUARY, FEBRUARY
- Production
- Proof Correction (I like to set these all out on the student desks when they come in and line up the kids. They go around the room and mark them all up for the submissions editor to check.)

MARCH
- Usually around this time the final book count, page count, and name tag list is due.

APRIL
- Begin to think about and prepare for end of year stuff... (see May / June above)
- Because we organize the Senior Superlaives (some schools call them mock elections... you know, "most likely to succeed") we host an awards show in our

auditorium called "The Senior Choice Awards". We have a red carpet and silly awards (for example, "Best All-Around" got a hoola hoop). We make a little money and it's fun.

MAY
- It starts all over again!
- End of the year: Never sign a senior's check-out card until his or her pages are absolutely completed. (This form is on page 117). Even the most dedicated students can't be counted on after they have exited your classroom and picked up their caps and gowns.

Kearsley High School Yearbook Staff

*&%$ Underhill Drive
Flint, Michigan 48506
Mrs. Kari Molter, Adviser
Yearbook Staff telephone: (810) 591-*&%$

• • • IMPORTANT INFORMATION • • •

Specifications for Senior Photographs in the
Kearsley Echo Yearbook

The Kearsley Echo Yearbook Staff requires the following type of senior picture. Photographs not meeting these requirements may not appear in the Kearsley Echo Yearbook. If you have any questions concerning these specifications, please contact Mrs. Kari Molter, Yearbook Adviser, at the above address or telephone number.

It is the responsibility of the student to see that his/her photographer delivers the required photograph to room 106 by the deadline date (November 1, 2008).

We require:
- one digital .jpg file on CD (preferred)
    or color glossy photograph
    1 1/2" (wide) x 2" (tall) in size
- head and shoulder pose ONLY
- inside or outside backround
- head size to be appropriate for the
    above size requirements
- **DEADLINE: NOVEMBER 1, 2007**

Courtesy of the Kearsley Adviser, Mrs. Kari Molter • June, 2008

Group Picture Day: December 19, 2007
Final Schedule

First Hour	Second Hour	Third Hour	Fourth Hour	Fifth Hour	Sixth Hour
* Class Officers * Special Olympics * National Honor Society	* Quiz Bowl * Chess * Women's Chorus	THIS HOUR ONLY THERE WILL BE TWO ANNOUNCE-MENTS. THE FIRST WILL BE 13 YEAR CLUB THEN THE REST OF THE SMALL GROUPS AFTER ABOUT 20 MINUTES. * Thirteen Year "Club" (only students who have attended KHS for all 13 years) ------- * Forensics * Thespian Society * Drama Club * Multicultural Club * Student Senate -------- * A Cappella Choir	* Newspaper * Broadcasting * Khorale * Harmonics	* Treble Singers * Club Latino * Inspired by God Bible Study * Tri-M Music Honor Society	* Yearbook * Concert Choir * DECA * Symponic Band * Wind Ensemble
Workers:	Workers:	Workers:	Workers:	Workers:	Workers:

Senior Check-Out Sheet

Seniors: You will not be checked out of my class until you have completed the following tasks. Give me this completed sheet with your check-out card.

1. Deadline (filled out by adviser):

___ All deadlines are complete.

___ The following deadlines must be completed.

Deadline Number	Topic	Completed (Molter Signature)

2. Box is cleaned out and inspected:

_____ Molter Signature

3. Name and Address where I can reach you over the summer:

Name: _____

Address: _____

City, State, Zip: _____

Home Phone: _____

Cell: _____

Underclassmen Check-Out Sheet

Seniors: You will not be checked out of my class until you have completed the following tasks:

1. Deadline:

___ All deadlines are complete.

___ The following deadlines must be completed.

Deadline Number	Topic	Completed (Molter Signature)

2. Box is cleaned out and inspected:

_____ Molter Signature

3. Name and Address where I can reach you over the summer:

Name: _____

Address: _____

City, State, Zip: _____

Home Phone: _____

Cell: _____

Notes:

CLASSROOM ENVIRONMENT

Classroom Environment

I like a classroom environment that is relaxed, yet businesslike. Team-Building activities are great, and pizza parties, ice cream parties, cheesecake parties when we meet deadlines keep them going.

It is important to keep the responsibility on the students, though… it is their responsibility to complete their pages on time. I love the saying, "Lack of planning on your part does not constitute an emergency on my part." You must be brutal about this.

There are a couple of team-building activities below, but I highly recommend the team-building books in the appendix.

The first is a nice get to know you activity, and the second is a good team-building activity using yearbook terms. I have unscrambled a few for you, but you should make your own, including things like your publisher's name and your sales representative's name. Do these team-building activities OFTEN… every day the first couple of weeks, then you can start spacing them out.

I have also done a word scramble with the names of everyone in the classroom in it. That's pretty fun.

As far as my classrooms set-up goes, I have a line of bookshelves on the back wall of my classroom that I have acquired over the years. Many of them are filled with yearbooks from our school as well as other schools. They are great to mine for layout and copywriting ideas. You can get these from your publishers sales representative.

On the top two shelves, I have a plastic box for each student. This is very handy for students to store their page folders, interview notes, and other materials. The picture on the previous page has the boxes stacked for the summer and other books on the bookshelves for storage. I normally have my students' boxes on the top two shelves during the school year. You don't have to invest in plastic boxes like I have. The tops from the boxes reams of paper come in can work, too.

I have two computers in my room… one on my desk for me and my submissions editor with the largest hard drive I could find, and another for my photography editor. These are the only two computers with the Adobe Photoshop program installed on them.

My staffers have a computer lab next door available to them.

Yearbook Adviser Survival Guide

Yearbook Autographs

Find someone in the group who has done any of the activities below and have that person sign his or her name in the block below. *** A person may only sign your sheet once***

Yearbook Word Scramble

Your job as a team is to unscramble the words below! You have 10 minutes! The team with the

Can speak a foreign language	Has been on TV or knows someone who has been on TV.	Has traveled to at least 10 other states	Would bungee jump if the chance occurred
Has had this class before	Has traveled by train	Knows what last year's (2004) yearbook theme was	Likes to read books
Looks most like you	Knows how to crop a photograph	Plays a musical instrument	Has met someone famous
Has performed on stage	Likes to ride horses	Likes roller coasters	Has more than two siblings
Has been to Mount Rushmore	Knows what a yearbook "flat" and "signature" is	Likes their dentist	Has a collection of some kind
Went to the yearbook workshop this summer	Has an unusual hobby	Knows what our yearbook theme for this year (2005) is.	Has earned service learning hours at KHS.

53

Yearbook Adviser Survival Guide

most unscrambled words wins a special prize!

Names _____

1	oldeub gpea rpsaed	Double page spread
2	ttuegr	
3	ntirnela rgmian	Internal margin
4	xlaeetnr aimgrn	External margin
5	tnanimod otohp	
6	mgiea lpecra	
7	atwshcse	
8	rkteos	
9	ypte oolt	
10	elestiocn ltoo	
11	gum tohs	Mug shot
12	iamge gat	Image Tag
13	owlsawthr lpibhnisug yomcpna	Walsworth Publishing Company
14	orna ungiey	
15	roopf	proof
16	boade esdgnnli	
17	rkeotmaw	
18	wcap ntosf	
19	olcnmsu	
20	ddrale aaidmrg	

THE MONEY GAME

The Money Game:
Selling Yearbooks and Selling Advertisements

Yearbook Sales

We sell yearbooks to a little over 50% of our school. In these economic times, we feel that this is pretty good, although we are always trying to improve our sales numbers.

Selling the books in August during summer registration is wonderful. The parents just walk down the line and write check after check... parking permit, lunch account, then one for the yearbook.

Our publisher also offers a website where we sell yearbooks as well. The number we sell this way increases every year.

Before I was the adviser at my school, parent volunteers would come and sell yearbooks at lunchtime.

Before we had August registration days, I would sell most of my books through the mail and a drop box in the office. We would mail sales flyers home and parents would mail them back to us with a check.

We sell probably 85% of our yearbooks at registration. The other 15% we sell via a mailer at the end of October or early November. We charge $5 more then. Then for those who wait until later in the school year we add another $5.

Below you will find the flyers we send out with the registration packets as well as a copy of our yearbook receipt. I go to a local print shop and have the order forms / receipts made up instead of using the ones provided by our publisher. It runs about $125 (for the 2012 school year), but saves much confusion later. In the past, I have used a three part NCR form, giving one to the purchaser as a receipt, saving one in numerical order for those parents who absolutely insist they bought a book when they really didn't (and can't produce a receipt), and then one we file the third in alphabetical order for easy pick-up. I am going to use a four-part form this year because we are having more and more students break up the cost of their yearbook into two payments and having a fourth receipt will allow me to easily accommodate this, giving out a receipt for the first and second payments.

Yearbook Adviser Survival Guide

How do you spell your name?
Your yearbook staff wants to know!

The yearbook staff wants to make sure your name is spelled correctly in the 2009 yearbook (whether or not you plan on purchasing one). Please let us know by filling in your name below and giving this form to the students working at the yearbook order table on your registration day. Shortened versions of your legal name are appropriate, but please, no nicknames. **Please write clearly in upper and lower case letters**.

Official Name in your Kearsley Records:

_____

Grade this fall: _____

How you would like your name to appear in the yearbook
upper and lower case letters, please print):

_____

Kearsley High School
2009 Yearbook Order Form and Receipt
Keep your receipt to present at yearbook distribution next year.

Last Name _____ First Name _____ Grade 9 10 11 12

Address _____ City _____

Zip _____ Telephone Number _____

☐ ONE All-Color Yearbook
Registration $60, November Sale $65, Late Purchases $70 $_____

☐ OPTION: Add Nameplate (same name as above) $5 $_____

☐ OPTION: Shipping (your yearbook will be mailed to you) $10 $_____

TOTAL: $_____

STAFF USE ONLY:
Remember to write the student's name on the memo line of the check! Give the last page of this to the purchaser as a receipt.

☐ Check #: _____   ☐ Cash   Staff Signature _____   Receipt #

This year will only happen once. You can't remember everything. The yearbook will remember it all for you!

KEARSLEY ECHO YEARBOOK REGISTRATION SALE!

The 2009 *ALL COLOR* yearbook will be on sale for the lowest price of the year at registration! Please fill out the order form below and bring a check or money order for the appropriate amount made out to "Kearsley Yearbook" to registration.
You will receive your receipt that day.

✂✂✂✂✂✂✂✂

Yearbook Order Form 2009 (Please Print)

Student Name: _____ Grade: _____

Address: _____ City _____

Zip _____ Phone Number _____

____ Yearbook: $60   ____ Nameplate: Add $5   ____ Shipping: Add $10

TOTAL: _____ Check Number: _____

Staff Use only: Receipt Number _____

Final Yearbook Sale!!

Your yearbook is the ONLY record of this school year...

This is your last chance to purchase a 2008 yearbook! Order yours now through November 16th!

Final Yearbook Sale Order Form

Mail to Kearsley High School Yearbook Staff 4302 Underhill Drive Flint, MI 48506
A receipt will be mailed to you.

Last Name _____ First Name _____ Grade _____

Address _____ City _____ Zip _____

Telephone Number _____

___ One All-color Yerbook $65 $65
___ Option: Add Nameplate $5   _____
___ Option: Shipping (your book will be mailed to you) $10   _____
                                               TOTAL: _____

Check # _____

Business Advertisements

I have to admit that this is my least favorite part of this job. When I was a kid I was so petrified of rejection that I made my sister sell my girl scout cookies door to door for me.

I hate dealing with advertising.

I know that there are schools that have really got it down. They sell thousands of dollars in advertising each year. We used to make about $10,000 in advertising each year between parent ads and business ads. At the moment we are struggling to hit $8000.

I don't have the magic solution for this, but here is what we do (or try to do). My business editor will spend a little time in her car at the beginning of the school year updating our business contact lists. These are a list of businesses, by location.

Our goal is to get a list of businesses in our area so my students won't have to drive around too much. They work in teams of two to three and visit each business on their list. We try to balance things out so each team has about the same number of businesses who have supported the book in the past.

We begin this process as early in the year as possible.

The goal for each student is usually around $300 between business ads and parent ads. I make it a grade. Meeting that individual goal will give the student 100/100 points. Going above that will earn other perks…

- $400 free yearbook
- For every $50 above that, the student earns one extra day on any deadline. This can come in very handy later on.

Giving a grade for selling advertisements is somewhat controversial at my school. I have been lucky to be supported by my administration on this, and, in truth, it is actually a small portion of a student's grade. Most of my students tell me that it really isn't hard to meet this goal, and compared to other schools, my per student goal is very low. (I know of one school where the goal is over $1000 per staffer.)

Because we have a fall book, we put together a simple brochure each year we call "The Blue and Gold Pages". We simply list the businesses by category that have advertised with us and distribute the flyer to all parents who attend parent-teacher conferences in the spring and the fall.

A different approach that I have not tried follows. I'm thinking about to putting the advertising pages earlier in the deadline set-up and the students who choose to design ad pages will be responsible for selling enough ads to fill their pages. We'll see how it goes. I may have to sell this to my students and so I plan on letting them know that the pages are pretty fun to design, one does not have to rely on coaches, lots of interviewing, or extensive body copy. There is virtually no copywritng or picture taking, and, with parent permission, they can leave the school during class time a limited number of days to sell ads. I will need to survey the kids beforehand to make sure there is enough interest amongst the staff to make this work. We'll see!

Four forms follow.

- The first is the advertising agreement we developed. It makes things easier than using a generic one from our publisher.
- The second is our billing letter we use to bill businesses.
- The third is a form my staffers fill out as they sell ads.
- The fourth is the flyer we send to our senior parents the same time as we send our final yearbook sale mailing letting them know about the parent ads. On the back of the form we will print one of our better parent ad pages from the previous year.

Yearbook Adviser Survival Guide

Kearsley High School
Kearsley Yearbook Advertising Agreement
Underhill Dr. Flint, MI 48506
Yearbook Staff Room: 591-####

Business Name _____ Phone _____

Business Address _____ City _____ Zip _____

Contact Name (print) _____ Authorized Signature _____

Rough Sketch of Layout

Ad Size (circle)
The Kearsley Echo proudly provides only all-color advertisements!
Whole Page	$350
Half Page	$250
1/4 Page	$150
1/8 Page	$80
Block (the size of this box)	$40

Specifications
___ Art/logo Furnished
___ Photo Required   taken: _____
___ Photo Furnished
___ Proof Requested   sent: _____
___ Other: _____

Payment
___ Cash $_____
___ Check # _____ $_____
___ Bill Company

Checklist- Staff Business Editor Only
1st Invoice Sent (date): _____ , 2nd Invoice Sent (date) _____
Payment Recieved (date): _____
Ad Salesperson: _____ Date Sold: ___/___/___
Staffer assigned: _____ Assigned to Page Number _____

White Copy- Advertising Editor
Yellow Copy- Page Designer
Pink Copy- Advertiser

Kearsley High School Yearbook Staff
Underhill Drive
Flint, MI 48506

Casey C&*%$#, Business Editor
591-####
January 5, 2008

INVOICE

Dear _____,

The Kearsley High School Yearbook Staff would like to thank you for supporting our yearbook.

We will work hard to produce a quality advertisement for your business as well as highlight your company in our "Gold Pages" which will be distributed in March to all high school parents.

In order to complete your advertisement, we are in need of the following:

PAYMENT INFORMATION:
____ Payment. Ad Size: _____ Amount Due: _____
____ No payment is necessary, your advertisement is paid in full. Thank-you.

ARTWORK:
____ We need your artwork or a description of what you would like us to create for you.
____ We have received your artwork. Thank-you.

We would appreciate it if you could please send payment as soon as possible. In order to be included in our "Blue and Gold Pages" booklet, we must have payment by the end of this month.

If you have any questions, please call me at the above number.
Sincerely,

Casey C&*%$#,
Business Editor
Kearsley High School Yearbook

Business Contact List

I have visited the following businesses with the following results:

Business Name	Contact Person	Date(s) Visited	Result: Yes/No	If yes, what?

Staffer(s): _____

Celebrate your child's journey through school...!

It's time to purchase a Senior Parent Advertisement in the yearbook!

1/8 page: $60 You may include one photo and up to 30 words of text.

1/4 page: $95 You may include as many as two photos and up to 60 words of text.

1/2 page: $175 You may include as many as three photos and up to 100 words of text.

Full Page: $280 The possibilities are endless!

Deadline: November 16th

Student Name _____

Ad Size: 1/8   1/4   1/2   Full Page

Amount Paid $_____   Check # _____

Mail this form with a check made out to "Kearsley Yearbook" to: KHS Yearbook Staff 4302 Underhill Drive Flint, MI 48506. Questions? Call Mrs. Molter at 591-5326. We prefer jpg digital photos. We can scan printed photos and will make every effort to return them to you if you write your name and complete address on the back of each photo.

Yearbook Sales at Registration

Instructions for Student Volunteers

NAME FORMS

All students and their parents will need to stop by and turn in the name form (the office has printed extras for us). You can use the silver basket for this. I wouldn't force people to fill one out, but if they don't it just means that we will use the name on their official records.

YEARBOOK ORDERS

It is pretty simple…

1. Have the people ordering yearbooks fill out their own name, grade, address, telephone number, and zip code. Make sure you have them fill out the order form NEATLY (THEY SHOULD PRINT) right at the table (don't let people take a form with them), and give out the forms in order so we know how many books we have sold.

2. They can then hand the order form to you with their check or money order made out to "Kearsley Yearbook". You write out the check number and the amount paid then sign your name on the "Authorized Signature" line.

3. Give them the pink copy and put the white and yellow copies in the black and white box.

Notes:

Yearbook Adviser Survival Guide

DIGITAL ORGANIZATON

Digital Organization

As I mentioned before, we currently use our publisher's Online Design program, and much of the organization of images is done for us. It is also nice that the students can work on their pages from home. In case you choose to use InDesign, here is what I used to do.

When we used Adobe In Design to produce our pages, it was important to organize all of these pages, so here is what I did… You will need to work closely with your school's network administrator to get this all set up.

ON THE NETWORK:

My classroom is located next door to a computer lab that is scheduled for journalism students all day. I assign each student to a computer.

I had our tech department give us our own "drive" on the network that ONLY yearbook students have access to. In this folder, I have several folders:
- Page Folders
    - We have 300 pages in our book, and create our pages in double-page spreads. I have my editors create a folder for each spread (DPS) so opening the "Page Folders" folder, you would see folders named
        - 1
        - 2-3
        - 4-5
        - 6-7
        - And so on…
    - Inside each page folder, we place an In Design layout with all of the required elements on it (folio tabs, page numbers, and layout requirements)
- Picture Folders
    - Inside this folder is a folder for each staff member.
    - My photo editor will place images into each student's folder as requested after they have been downloaded from the cameras, corrected, and requested by the student.
- Click Art
    - Our publisher provides us with click art, so my students access it here.

The students are reminded to back-up their files regularly to the hard drive of the computer they have been assigned.

ON THE PHOTO COMPUTER

I have two computers in my classroom: one on my desk and another that we use as our photo computer. I'm concerned about having the same picture appear over and over in the yearbook, so I have my photo editor download the cameras and keep the photos organized by subject.

Then my staffers can get on that computer and choose the photographs they want to use on their pages. My photo editor approves those choices (they must be good pictures… clear, interesting, etc.) and transfers the photos to the correct student's photo folder.

ON THE COMPUTER ON MY DESK:

This is the computer that my submissions editor uses.

When an entire deadline is completed, my submissions editor copies all of the page folders into a "Completed Pages" folder I placed on my desktop. It is from there that all future changes are made. She creates PDF files, then re-opens those pages to make proof corrections as well.

I use the little half sheet form on the following page as a tool for my photo editor, so we have a record of when a photo was requested and when it was moved. It cuts down on the "blame game".

Please move these pictures to my folder!

Name _____ Today's Date _____

Folder Name where the picture is located:

Picture Names (example: DSCF1234) (do not ask to have all of the pictures moved… maximum 10 pictures per request):

_____
_____
_____
_____
_____

_____
_____
_____
_____
_____

Date completed: _____ by _____
Make sure the moved pictures are renamed "used"

Yearbook Adviser Survival Guide
YEARBOOK DISTRIBUTION

Distribution

Because we are a fall book, yearbook distribution has always been somewhat of a challenge. In the past, we have delivered most of our books at Homecoming.

In the past, we have set up a booth in the choir room whose back door is conveniently located yards away from the entrance to the football stadium. (Unfortunately this room is as far away as one can get from the yearbook staff room so we had to cart the boxes and boxes of books there ourselves that day.)

I scheduled my staffers for a one hour shift that night, about four staffers per hour, and we distributed about 80% of our books at that time.

It worked out well, except for a few busy times when there was a line.

We would ask for identification and have the student sign the back of the order form then give him or her the book.

The registration days are great for us. The school schedules about 2 ½ hours in the morning and 2 ½ hours in the afternoon over two days… each grade level would have a slot in which they would have their school pictures taken, pay for their parking permit, pay into their lunch account, buy their yearbook (!) and pick up their yearbook from the previous year.

BASIC TRAINING
(Teacher Packet)

Basic Training

What follows is my staff handbook. I have included the answers for you after the student packet.

Every year I try to make the staff training shorter, but it still seems to take about about six weeks to train my rookie staffers in the basics. They learn a lot of it "on the job" as they work on their pages but what follows is my attempt to get them started…

There is wonderful information available through your publisher or the various journalistic resources at the end of the book. Again, this is just what has worked well for me.

📖 Yearbook Class Handbook 📖

Kearsley High School

Staffer: _____

📖 Yearbook Class Handbook 📖

Course Outline
- Introduction, Syllabus
- The Basics of Yearbook Journalism
- Copywriting
- Layout / Computers
- Choose Deadlines
- Production (The rest of the year)

Grading (after basic training)

For each deadline you will have the potential to earn 300 points. Near the beginning of the year, you will have the opportunity to choose the yearbook pages you will be working on. This will result in somewhere between six and eight deadlines.

* One third of your grade will be determined according to the date your deadline IS ACCEPTED. "Accepted" means that all editors have signed your check sheets and the entire package is accepted by me (Mrs. Molter). More often than not, I will then tell you what you need to fix... you make the corrections, and then get it back to me. YOU WILL NOT EARN A GRADE UNTIL I SAY THAT THE DPS IS ACCEPTABLE.

* The second third of your grade will be determined by the accuracy of your work. It is incredibly important for us to be accurate when it comes to facts and names. Do you want your name to be spelled wrong in the book? Of course not; every one of the 1200 students in this school feels the same way. For each incorrectly spelled or inaccurate name on your page or in your index, you will lose 10 points from this category. Unsubstantiated quotes (quotes without attached pages from your reporter's notebook signed by the interviewee) will also cause you to lose 10 points per problem. Inaccurate scoreboards will also cause you to lose points. Print out a copy of the scoreboard from the KHS website the day you turn it in to me.

* The final third of your grade will be determined by your creativity. How interesting is your copy? Your captions? Are your pictures clear and show people's faces? Is your layout interesting, creative, different? Work with your team leader to get comfortable with InDesign so you can do some fun things with your pages.

My best advice to you is to do your work early. If you are having a problem with a deadline, (it is a problem beyond your control) you are to inform me IN WRITING at least ONE MONTH before your deadline date of the problem. Include the page numbers, deadline date, date you are informing me and the nature of the problem. You and I will conference about this problem and come up with an acceptable solution which may (but may not) include an adjusted deadline.

Be aware that people take forever to return information sheets. I DO NOT recommend this method of gathering information from anyone on any subject. Interview people. Talk to them. Don't be shy. Listen for an interesting story. You can't get that from a sheet of questions.
Sports pages take time, probably more time than any other page. Coaches are notoriously UNhelpful. You MUST begin early trying to get information from them. Listen to the announcements and gather information from that. They are posted in the office window. Read them. Also, it will be incredibly difficult to get meaningful quotes concerning any events months after the event has occurred (for example, trying to get quotes about football season in February when you are actually working on that page).

I will be very unforgiving when it comes to late deadlines. You MUST plan ahead and let me know of a problem early. Having done this for nearly 20 years, I know that there are very few legitimate excuses.

If you feel that you do have a legitimate excuse, however, you must submit a letter to me (Yes, IN WRITING) when giving me your final page packet explaining why your work is late and why it was beyond your control. Just so you know, the following excuses are unacceptable: I was absent, I had to work so I couldn't get the pictures, we had a snow day, I had to wait for the editor to check my work, I asked Stacy (or Kim or Mrs. Molter) to take my pictures and they didn't do it or they did a terrible job. GET YOUR WORK DONE EARLY! STAY AFTER SCHOOL... GIVE YOURSELF HOMEWORK!

The grading scale is as follows:
- Acceptance **before** your deadline date: "A" with exam exemption credit (100 pts)
- Acceptance on your deadline date: "A" with no exam exemption credit (100)
- Acceptance one day late: "A-" (92)
- Acceptance two days late: "B+" (89)
- Acceptance three days late: "B" (86)
- Acceptance four days late: "B-" (82)
- Acceptance five days late: "C+" (79)
- After FIVE days, your DPS will be given to your section editor, and you will earn an "E" in all areas (0)

Other details about your grade...

1. The first quarter may also include quizzes or assignments on yearbook skills and/or a project.

2. I reserve the right to adjust your grade or revoke exam exemption at any time if I feel that your classroom behavior warrants this action.

3. First quarter, you will be selling advertisements and promoting the marketing of the book will be a part of your grade. It will count as much as a deadline grade. Your goal will be $300. If you earn $400 you will receive a free yearbook, and for every $50 above that, you will earn a certificate for an extra day on a deadline. There may be other fundraisers as well. You will be expected to contribute to this aspect of our business.

Editors

Your editors have all spent at least one year on the staff already. They know what they are doing. Let them help you. If, at any time, you are not treated with respect by any editor, you are expected to let your adviser know. They are, however, responsible for keeping you on track for meeting your deadlines, so accept their help, ask for it, and do your best. They are responsible for letting your adviser know how you are doing, so they are not being nosy, they are trying to help us all meet our deadlines.

Semester Grades

Semester grades will be determined using a point system. Each deadline will be worth 300 points. The first quarter grade will be counted as a percentage and will be worth 40% of the final grade, the second quarter grade will be counted as a percentage and will be worth 40% of the final grade, and the exam will be counted as a percentage and will be worth 20% of the final grade.

Exam Exemption

As a reward for completing your work early, you can be granted exemption from your mid-term and final exams. It is very important that you keep this page and have it signed when you earn exemption from your exam. My records will not be able to tell if you have earned exemption, so please keep close track of this page.

Deadline 1   Due: _____   Completed: _____   Teacher Signature: _____

Deadline 2   Due: _____   Completed: _____   Teacher Signature: _____

Deadline 3   Due: _____   Completed: _____   Teacher Signature: _____

Deadline 4   Due: _____   Completed: _____   Teacher Signature: _____

Deadline 5   Due: _____   Completed: _____   Teacher Signature: _____

Deadline 6   Due: _____   Completed: _____   Teacher Signature: _____

Deadline 7   Due: _____   Completed: _____   Teacher Signature: _____

Deadlines

Record your deadlines here. Be absolutely accurate.

Deadline	Date Due	Page No's	Subject	Special Instructions
1				
2				
3				
4				
5				
6				
7				

Schedule

Below is the schedule we will follow as you are taught the basics of copywriting, layout, and computers. I will move quickly, but I will not allow you to go into production until I feel you have mastered this information.

You must master a significant amount of information before moving on to production. The more closely you study the material, take part in our discussion, and work through the assignments, the quicker the lessons will be done and you will have the skills necessary to produce a quality publication.

YOU MUST COMPLETE YOUR PRACTICE ASSIGNMENT BEFORE YOU CAN MOVE INTO PRODUCTION.

THE BASICS OF YEARBOOK JOURNALISM

Pay attention to the demonstrations and lectures. Grab a yearbook from the shelf for today's lecture. Take notes here, making sure to define important terms in a way that makes sense to you (you might want to draw a picture).

- A yearbook is a cross between a _____magazine_____ and a _____newspaper_____.

- The four functions of a yearbook are:

    - **Memory Book**: capture everyone's memories… not just the popular kids. What makes this year special?

    - **Reference Book**: Names, scoreboards, facts must be accurate. Our local police department requests a book every year to identify people.

    - **Public Relations Tool**: Students, principals, parents, community members look at this book. Be real, but with a positive general attitude. Don't lie, or pretend all is perfect, but when you have the choice, focus on the positive. Don't seek out the negative.

    - **History Book**: Include historical events (like the election) as well as school-related items. This book should be dated… pages like fashion are very interesting to look at in the future.

- Other important terms:
    - Ladder: A list of the contents of each page of the yearbook.

    - Theme: A unifying element in every yearbook.

- Signature: 16 pages of the yearbook folded into a booklet. These booklets get bound together to form the complete book.

- Flat: 8 pages or one half of a signature

- Title Page: First page in the yearbook after the front endsheets, gives basic school information and introduced the theme.

- Division Pages: Divides the book into sections. For us it's fall, winter, spring, and summer.

- Endsheets: Hold the pages of the book to the cover.

- Opening / Closing Sections: Pages that begin and end the book by developing its theme.

- Index: A listing of the name and page number where a student is pictured in the yearbook.

- Colophon: The last page of the book. This gives publication information.

- Sections of the book / Types of pages:
  - Student Life: feature stories on happenings inside and outside the school. (Look at other yearbooks for these types of pages). Examples include homecoming, fashion, etc.
  - Academics / Clubs and Organizations: These pages cover all of these groups in the school as well as happenings within classes.
  - Sports: Varsity, JV, and Freshman sports
  - Mugs: Student pictures (head and shoulder shots)
  - Community: Advertising

- How important is a theme and where does it get developed in a book? Important for unity within the book. It gets developed on the cover, by the page number (folio tabs), on the endsheets, on the title page, on division pages, and subtly on most spreads in the book.

- Legal Issues. Define the following terms and how they are important to you as a yearbook staffer:
  - First Amendment to the Constitution of the United States: Freedom of Speech

- Tinker Ruling: This court case protected students' first amendment rights. See this informative website:
  http://www.firstamendmentschools.org/resources/handout1a.aspx?id=13968

- Hazelwood Ruling: This court case allowed censorship of student publications with "reasonable educational justification". See this website for a summary:
  http://www.splc.org/law_library.asp?id=1

- Copyright: We cannot use song lyrics, copyrighted characters, or that type of thing in the yearbook without permission.

- Libel: False written statement about a person.

- Privacy: students deserve their privacy. If they don't want something in the yearbook, they have the right to ask us not to print it.

- Obscenity: be careful of things like photographs that may be looked at as inappropriate. One place this could happen is on a page about a school dance where girls might be wearing low cut dresses and the pictures could be taken as inappropriate.

COPYWRITING

> **Activity: With a partner, look in some of our old yearbooks and yearbooks from other schools. Find interesting copy… story copy, captions, and headlines. As a group, we will share and discuss what makes the writing good. Be ready to contribute your findings.**

Prewriting

Who are our potential readers? Everyone!

What aspects of students lives should be covered? Pretty much all aspects, keeping in mind the students' right to privacy.

Do you ever give YOUR opinion? No, never.

Ways to get information for your pages:
- Clippings (info from school announcements)
- Poll or survey
- Research
- Interviewing

Interviewing

Your articles will be created by gathering interesting quotations from students and staff then placing them in your article that gives all the necessary facts in an interesting way. Therefore, interviewing is an extremely important skill to learn.

- **The Interviewing Process:**
    1. Make an appointment
    2. Prepare questions ahead of time
    3. Write down key facts, not every word
    4. Verify direct quotes
    5. Organize notes immediately after the interview
    6. Last question: Do you have anything you want to add?

- The "5 W's and one H" are the basis for any interview and article. Make sure you find out the WHO, WHAT, WHEN WHERE, WHY, and HOW about your topic.
- <u>The better the questions, the better the quotes.</u>

- **Questions <u>to avoid</u> in an interview:**
  - No leading questions (ie. How much did you hate losing out as homecoming queen ?)
  - No "feelings" questions (ie. How did you feel when you were crowned queen?)
  - No yes/no questions (you don't get good quotes that way)

- **You DO want STORYTELLING QUOTES.**
  - Concentrate on the human interest aspect
    - *How did you benefit from* your community service work?
  - Ask questions that will make the person think
    - *What was the most satisfying aspect of* being a peer leader?
    - *What was the most frustrating* aspect?
    - *What would you have done differently?*
    - *Why are you active in this club?*

Writing Body (Story) Copy

General Information

Your body copy must be written in past tense. Why, you ask? It's simple. When the book is delivered in the fall, all of the events have happened already… in the past. Thus, past tense.

Each paragraph will contain no more than two sentences. This is why… our columns are not very wide. Any more than two sentences will make your article difficult to read.

Deliver the 5 W's and 1 H. In twenty years, the details of an event will have been lost. It's your job to preserve them for the whole school. Think back to the four purposes of a yearbook… why you are doing this. It's to preserve the *history* of this year, serving as a *record* of the events, keep the memories, and show the community

Don't just say "said". Check out the pages in this handbook that suggest other ways to say this word. Just make sure you are using an appropriate word. Connotation is important.

Quote-Transition Format and the Cut-Off Test

In the simplest of terms, your body copy must tell the story of an event or a season in an interesting way. It is your job to bring the moments to life so people who read the book in twenty years will feel like they are there again.

Articles are written in **Quote-Transition Format**. This is why you need good, storytelling quotes. This is a simple process, really. Interview people about your page, then choose the best quote, next best quote, next best quote and so on until you get to the worst one. Write your article using your best quote first then the least interesting and/or informative quote at the end.
This is important because you may need to cut off the end of your article when you place it onto your page. If your least interesting / informative quotes are at the end of your article, you won't lose any important information or have to totally rewrite your article. An article that is written in this manner will pass the **cut-off test** and make your job easier.

The Lead

You will begin your article with a lead. A lead is brief, creative, and original. It is meant to make your reader want to read the rest of the article. You are trying to catch the reader's attention with your lead. Below are several types of leads you can use. We will discuss the examples and then look for some more in old yearbooks for you to add yourself.

- **3 or 4 well-chosen words**

    Gasoline, oil, cookies, perm solution... these are just a few smells students encountered at the Genesee Area Skill Center.

    School, sports, after-school jobs, money, and family all seem to stress the average high school student, considering every student has obligations and responsibilities to live up to in and out of school.

    Barbie dolls that walk, Nerf guns with extra power, fuzzy stuffed animals that you can teach to talk, all of these things have young adults making stops at their local toy store.

    Pogo Voodoo, Big Apple, Food Processor, Shooting Butterfly... is this a new foreign language? (article on hacky-sacks)

    _____
    _____
    _____
    _____

- **A description using sensory details**

    The sky was dark and pierced by lightening; the rain fell steadily as cheers erupted from the stands and the announcers told jokes. Everything was the same as the average Friday night football game—except it was Monday, and the girls ruled the field.

    The television set clicked on and all eyes were focused on the screen. It was the beginning of fifth hour and the announcements were about to begin.

    The score was 18-20 with the jayvee hornets down by two; Three seconds were left in the game. All Kearsley needed for a victory against Clio was a field goal.

    _____
    _____
    _____
    _____

- **An unusual or thought-provoking question**

   Are your friends dependable? Are they there for you when you need them? Well, many friends at KHS are.

   Mix together 16 veteran cheerleaders, two new coaches, and a new mascot. Whay do you get?

   _____
   _____
   _____

- **An interesting quote**

   " The players had the talent, tradition, and ability to do their best and win," quoted Mr. Mike Smith, and he was absolutely right.

   " If I could change anything about myself, it would be my attitude. Sometimes I have a bad attitude towards my family and it really is not nice of me to act like that, because they don't deserve it," stated Kristy O'Brien.

   _____
   _____
   _____

- **A summary**

   The Varsity Softball team has been on a ten year winning streak, but unfortunately that all changed this year.
   Service learning was a great way for Kearsley students to reach out to the community.

   They were exposed to new people and things that may not have been a part of their everyday lives. Many of the students enjoyed the feeling that they got when they made someone smile.

   The Kearsley Chess team had an incredible season filled with many highlights and achievements. The Chess team tied for first in the league with Powers in addition to taking first and second in two different State Championship meets.

   _____
   _____
   _____

- **A teaser**

    The lights went dim. the audience finished up their last conversation until intermission, and the curtain was lifted. Already standing on the stage were actors Kedree Olds (Mugsy) Randy Houghton (Legs) and Adam Washington (Dan Bartone).

    It was Christmas time at Kearsley, and Mr. Jones' third hour political science class was acting as Santa Claus.

    Teachers, imagine this: You open your classroom door after the room has been occupied by another class. As you turn on the lights you notice every one of your desks has been turned upside down in the middle of the classroom. Is it a case of desk vandalism? Why no, it's a teacher prank!

    _____
    _____
    _____
    _____

A Sample Article (annotated)

Shake and Fake

The lights dimmed and the crowd grew silent. Seconds later, as the stage lit up, you would think someone would start singing, but that wasn't the case.	(quote)
This was the annual Lip Sync Contest and to win, you simply had to fake it. Returning three-time champ Brad Gilleland was one of the crowd's favorites.	(transition)
"I tried to work the crowd the best I could, but obviously that didn't work out too well" Gilligan exclaimed. "It's not so much that I placed second, because I'm a good sport; a lot of people came up to me afterwards and told me I should have won, but it's okay… you win some, you lose some.	(quote)
Even with the reigning champ at hand, some acts prepared heavily for the contest while others basically winged it on stage.	(transition)
"I wasn't prepared at all because I hadn't planned on doing it and I put it together the night before" Leah Blakenship confessed.	(quote)
This year, Gilleland was dethroned by Alex Groban and Brianna Desrochers. Even with the winning act, Groban said they had a rough time choosing a song to perform.	(transition)
"We were going to do "What I've Been Looking For" then Brianna called me and said that she had a dream and she wanted to do "My Humps" Groban explained. "Then we decided to not do that song s we chose "Breaking Free" because we knew that one would be a crowd pleaser."	(quote)

(There is more to this article, but you get the idea, right? Quote, transiton, quote, transition, quote, transition.)

Concluding your article

- Do not write a conclusion. Just end your article with a quotation and be done with it. Why? Remember the cut-off test? You might have to cut off the end of your article to make it fit into the space you have available. Another reason to NOT write a conclusion is that you have a limited amount of space in which to present your event. Use that space to show what happened.
- Do not write about the future as you conclude your article. Talk about what happened this year, not what might happen in the future.
- Another temptation to resist is praising the team. (Great season, guys!) That's giving your opinion and it must be avoided.

Headlines

- All good headlines are specific, positive, and free of editorializing.
- They tell the reader something important, don't just serve as a label
- Write them in past tense.
- They present a complete thought in descriptive nouns and strong verbs. Use adjectives sparingly.
- They don't rehash the article's lead.
- They don't state the obvious (such as the school's name, mascot, year, or group name)
- Don't use words such as "students" or "seniors"
- Do not use the words "a", "an", or "the"
- Instead of the word "and" use a comma
- Use single, not double quotes

- Avoid copying song or movie titles
- Subheads expand on the headline, give more information. They might appear above or below a headline.
- Some examples of good headlines (we'll go through old yearbooks to find more):

Stir or Snooze
Personal choices and academic pressures dictate the schedules of early risers and late sleepers.

• •

Tough mental attitude
carries swimmers through
season to fifth
place at state

Pulling Through

Trendy Toys
Rollerblades, Koosh balls, and *Assassin* replace hackey sacks and *Pictionary*.

Captions
- Must provide the answers to questions readers will have about the photo (who, what, when, where, and especially the why and how.)
- Each caption must be at least two sentences long.
  - First sentence: present tense, what is happening in the photo
  - Second sentence: past tense, tell additional information... more than the obvious.
- Captions must tell more than the obvious. What happened before and after the picture was snapped? (Hint: take your own pictures and take notes when you take them... 5 W's and 1 H plus what happened before and after... what was the outcome of the game... did the guy hit a home run or strike out?)
- All people in the photos must be identified with first and last names.
- In group shots, use the following format:
- Back row: Sally Jones, Joe Forman, and Ron Mantle. Front row: Bill Card, Jim Smith. (Always begin in the back. There is no need to indicated left to right.)
- Teachers should be referred to in this format: Mrs. Kari Molter
- <u>Do not</u> indicate the graduation year of the students (ie. Sophomore Jimmy Neutron)
- Some examples of good and bad captions (we'll search out more in old yearbooks, too.)

  - Good and bad: **Mr. Walth presses the new discipline plan into Eric Hule's mind. Mr. Walworth left a lasting impression on many students this year.** (Echo 2000, p.7) (Good: the picture had Mr. Walworth standing with one foot on Eric while talking into his walkie-talkie. The word "presses" in the first sentence is good, it fits with the picture, and the student's full name is there. The first sentence fits with the theme of the page, the new discipline system. Bad: the second sentence is a filler. It tells nothing new, adds no important information to the caption.)

  - Good: **Inspired by the music groups ICP and Twiztid, Brett Ayer shows off his bright red hair. Later in the year, Ayers was seen showing off his hair in a bright blue color.** (Echo 2000, p.9) (The first sentence is in present tense and names the student in the photo as well as gives interesting information... why he colored his hair. The second sentence, in past tense, gives more information, tells more than the obvious.)

  - Terrible: **Captain Melissa Pake is putting. She was practicing for a match.** (Echo 2000, p.177). (This is a totally obvious caption. You guessed it, the girl in the picture is putting. The writer needed to do more research here. She could have interviewed the girl and gotten a quote for this caption to add more information than just the obvious. She could have done more research and found out how the girl contributed to the team. Another thing the person creating the page could have done is get to the matches and take better pictures instead of just settling for posed shots.)

- Excellent: **The Owosso defense looks on with astonishment as Emily Androswky heads in the tying goal in the district semifinals. Emily had three goals and five assists throughout the season.** (Echo 2000, p.179). (This is one of those captions that is helped because the picture is great. The staffer went to games and made sure to get great pictures. Because of this, she was able to capture an important moment in an important game. The first sentence is good because it identifies the team we were playing against and the center of attention in the photo… Emily Androwski. The photo tells why this was an important moment. The second sentence adds important information about this player.)

- Terrible: **With Joseph Veneguhs we thought we were in Vegas. He was the ace up our sleeve.** (Echo 1996 p.14). (It's a football page. The caption starts its first sentence with a stupid rhyme which gives little information about what he is doing, who he's playing against, etc. It is in past tense, which is also a problem. The second sentence tells nothing. It's pure filler.)

Layout

Good Photographs
- Capture the action and reaction, expression and emotion of a moment.
- They reach out to readers and tell stories that captions, headline and body copy complete.
- Have a story to tell.
- Capture a reader's attention.
- Are clear, not blurry
- ZOOM WITH YOUR FEET! GET CLOSE TO THE ACTION!
- Cover from all angles.
- Think UNIQUE and EXCITING!
- Check out some good and bad examples from yearbooks…

Layout

Before you can even begin to create the layout for a page, there are some terms you must get used to.

- Dominant photo: The largest photo on the page. It gets the attention of the person right away when he or she looks at the page.

- Two-page spread (DPS): Double Page Spread. We look at the facing pages of a spread as one thing, not two separate pages.

- External Margins: White space on the outside of a page.

- Internal Margins: The distance between elements on a apage.

- Columns: Many good basic layouts use a column format. We will practice this.

- Eyeline: An internal margin that goes across both pages to draw the reader's eye across the page.

- Rule Lines: Lines around pictures or lines on a page for a design purpose.

- Screens: blocks of color or grey on a page.

Basic Layout Rules

1. Start with a dominant photo that is at least 2 ½ times larger than any other photo on the spread. Place it toward the center of the page.

2. Other Pics: 3-7 per page (try to make different shaped photo boxes, some long, some tall, some square), place them toward the center of the page.

3. One grid internal margins, create an eyeline.

4. Captions: stack no more than 2. Place them on the corners of your layout. They must touch the picture to which they belong.

Basic Layout

Column Format

This is the most basic type of layout. Once you have some time to practice this, then you can expand to more complicated types of layout such as grid design and modular design.

Keep in mind that this is very basic layout. Color, photo choice, and font choice are not addressed here. A good exercise is to pick apart appealing layouts from other yearbooks and, later, magazines, to analyze their layout technique.

1. Begin with a double page spread (two facing pages).

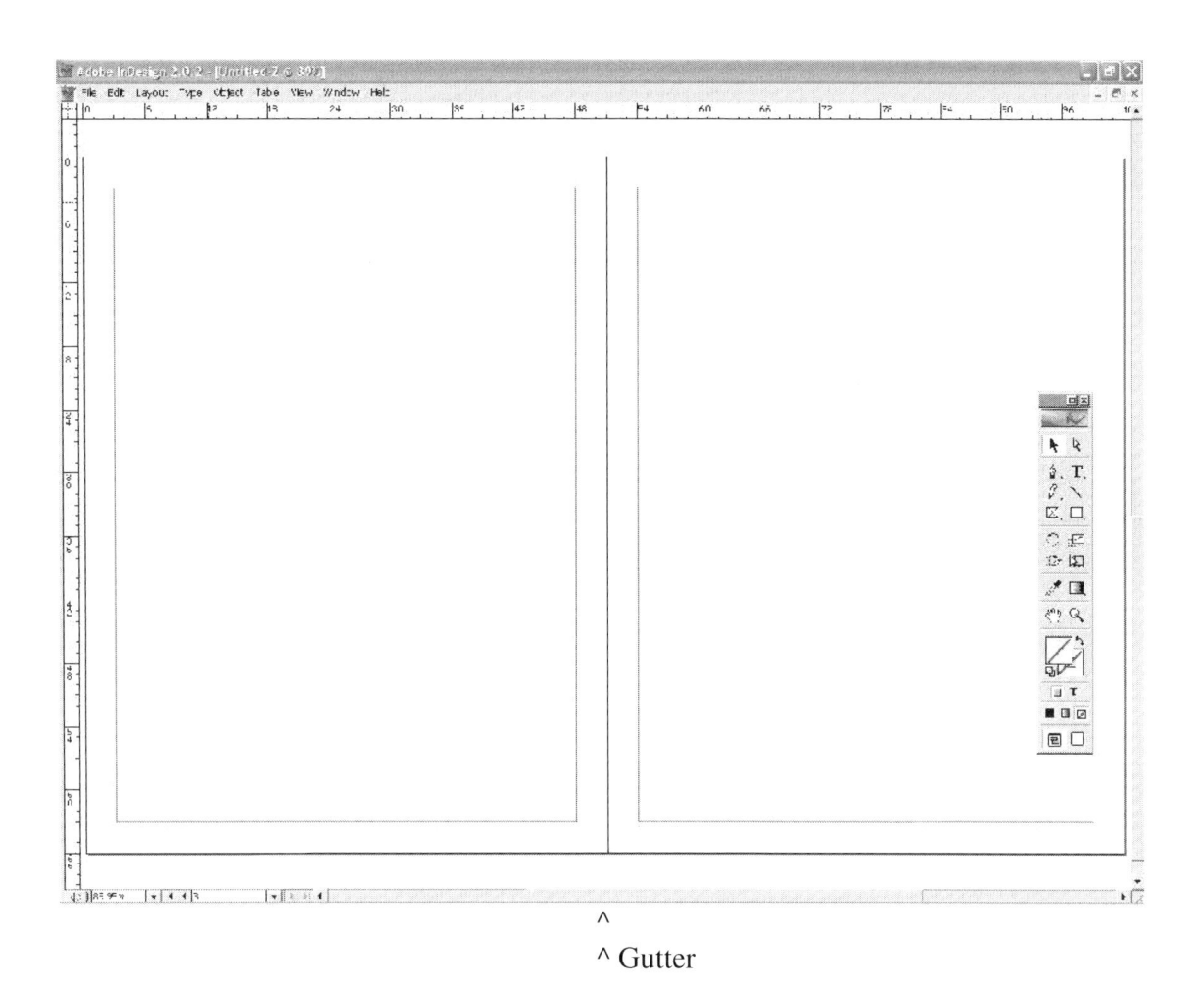

^
^ Gutter

2. Chose the number of Columns You wish to use. Typical column formats are three, four, and five. The following example is a four-column format… four columns on each side. The key is always stopping and starting on a column line.

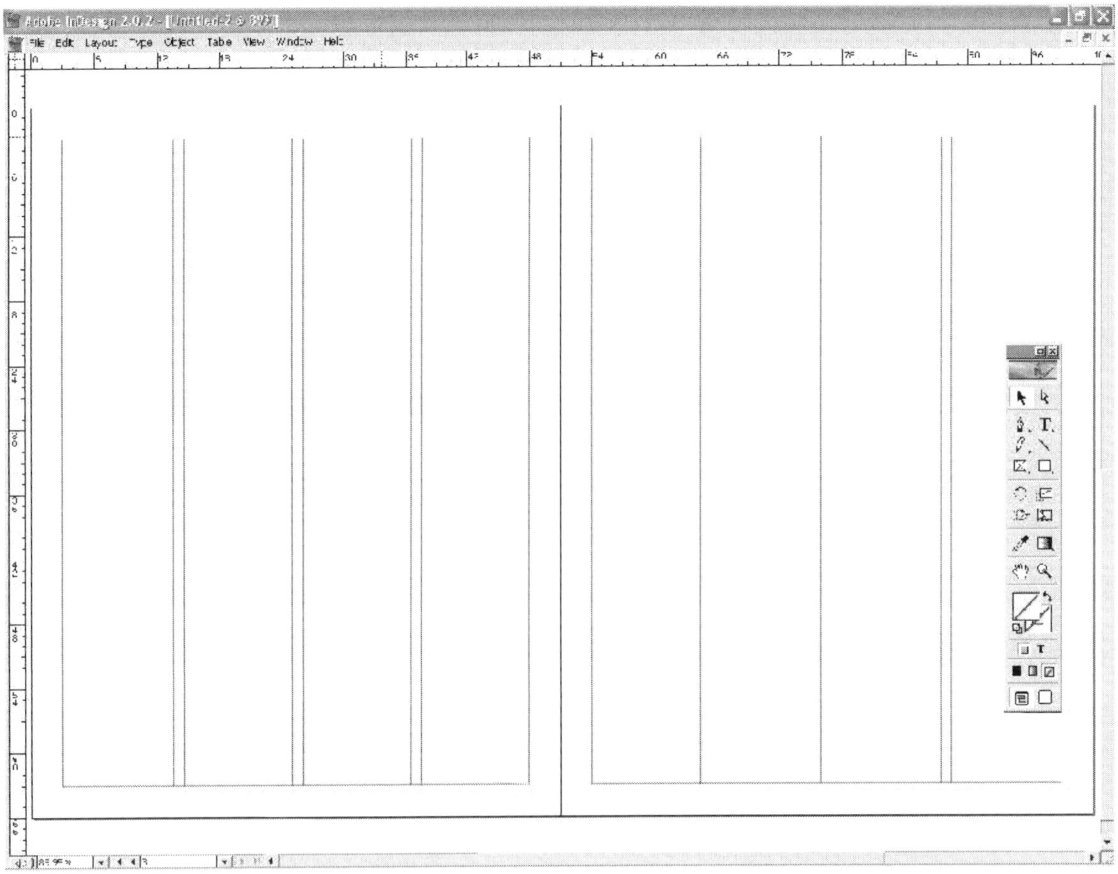

^ ^ ^ ^
column column

Note that the first column ends then a new column starts. Note where the photos and copy begin and end on the following examples as the layout develops. They always end at the edge of a column. Photos and copy can be more than one column wide, but they always begin and end on a column line.

3. Place a dominant photo near the center of the layout, crossing the gutter to tie the two halves of the page together.

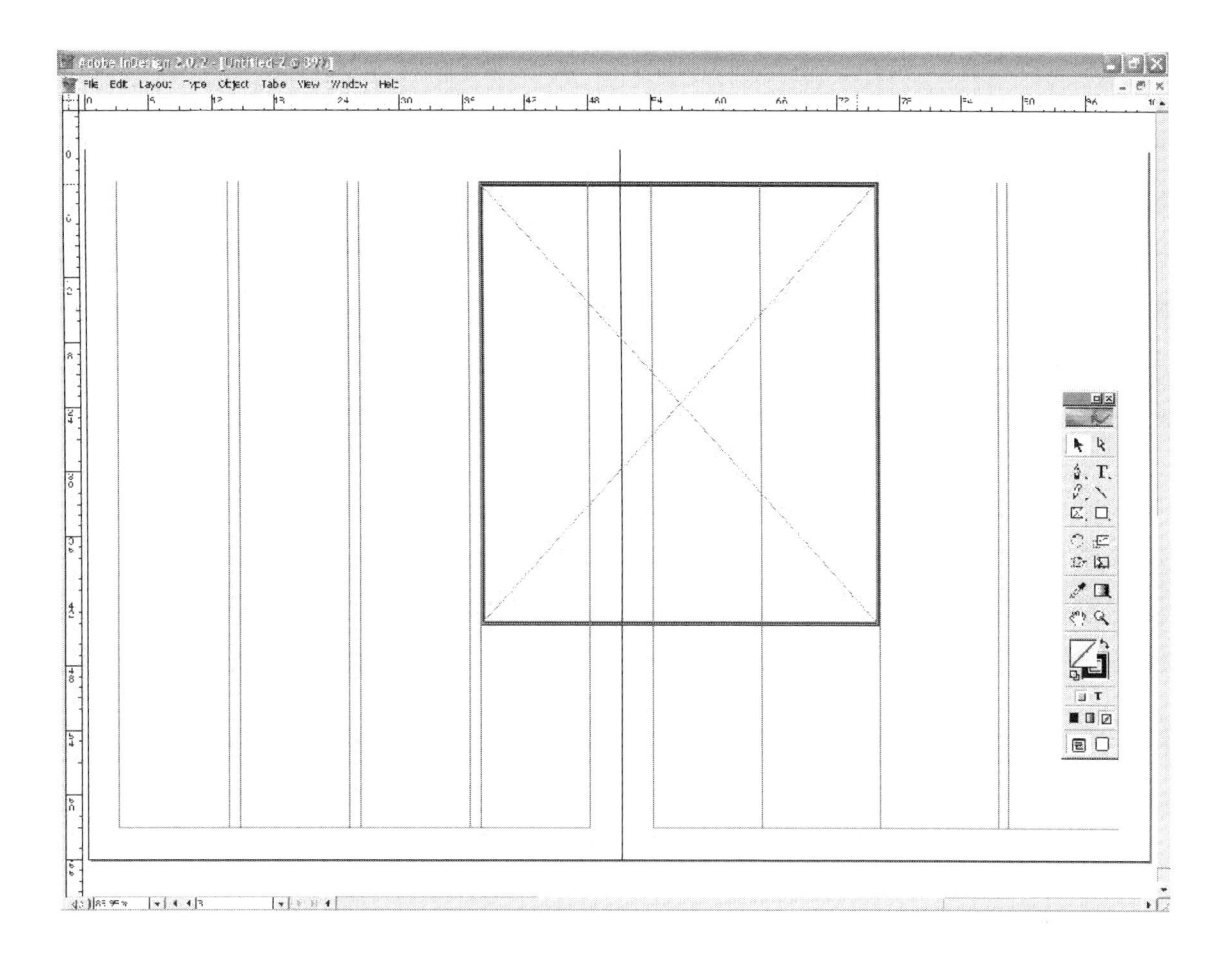

4. Place other photos around the dominant photo… create an eye line. (In this case, the eye line will be below this photo. Use consistent internal margins (space between all photos) and leave room for a headline and body copy as well as captions (which go best on the corners). Use a variety of picture shapes.

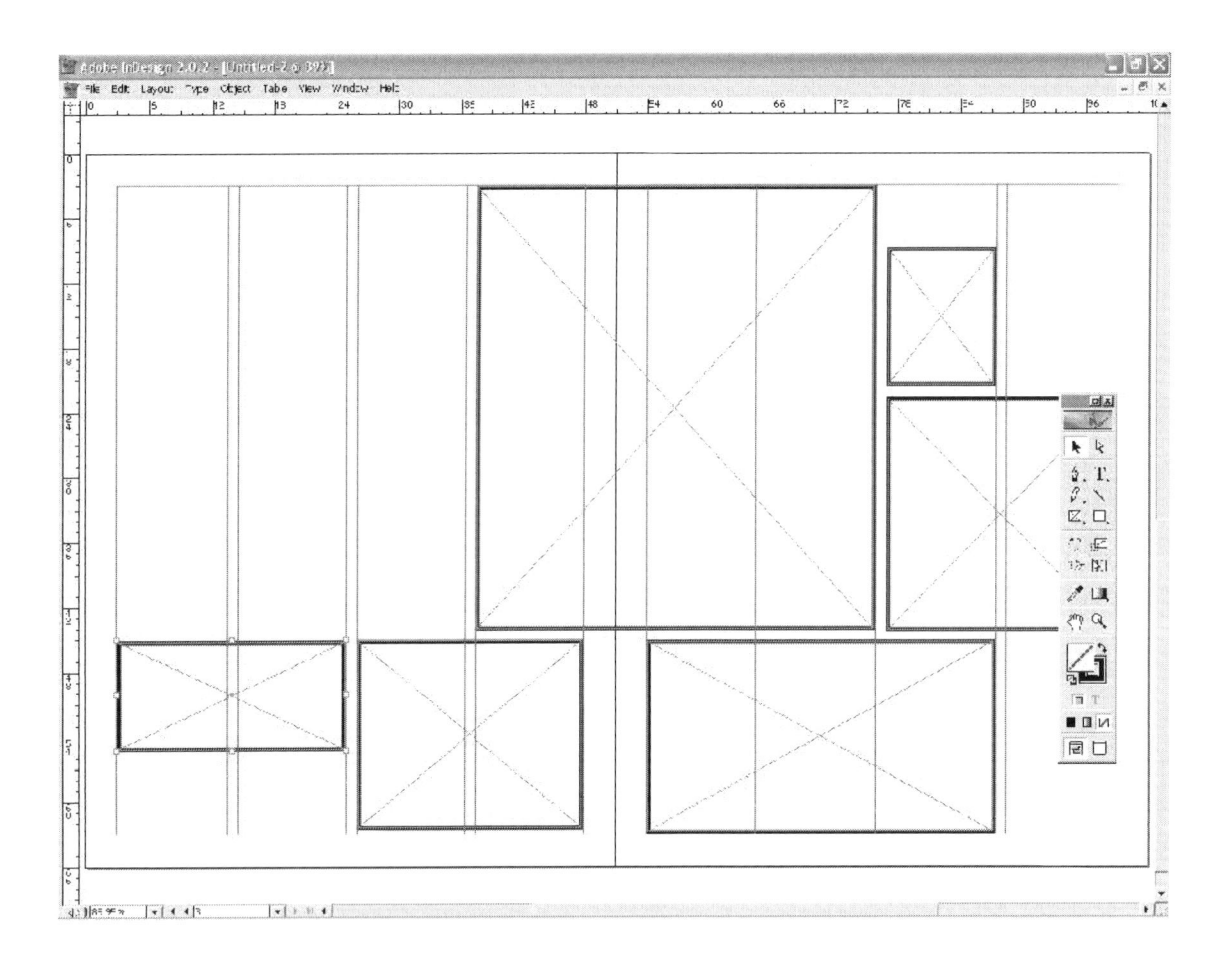

5. Place captions on your layout so they touch the photo to which they belong. Stack no more than two captions. Keep consistent internal margins.

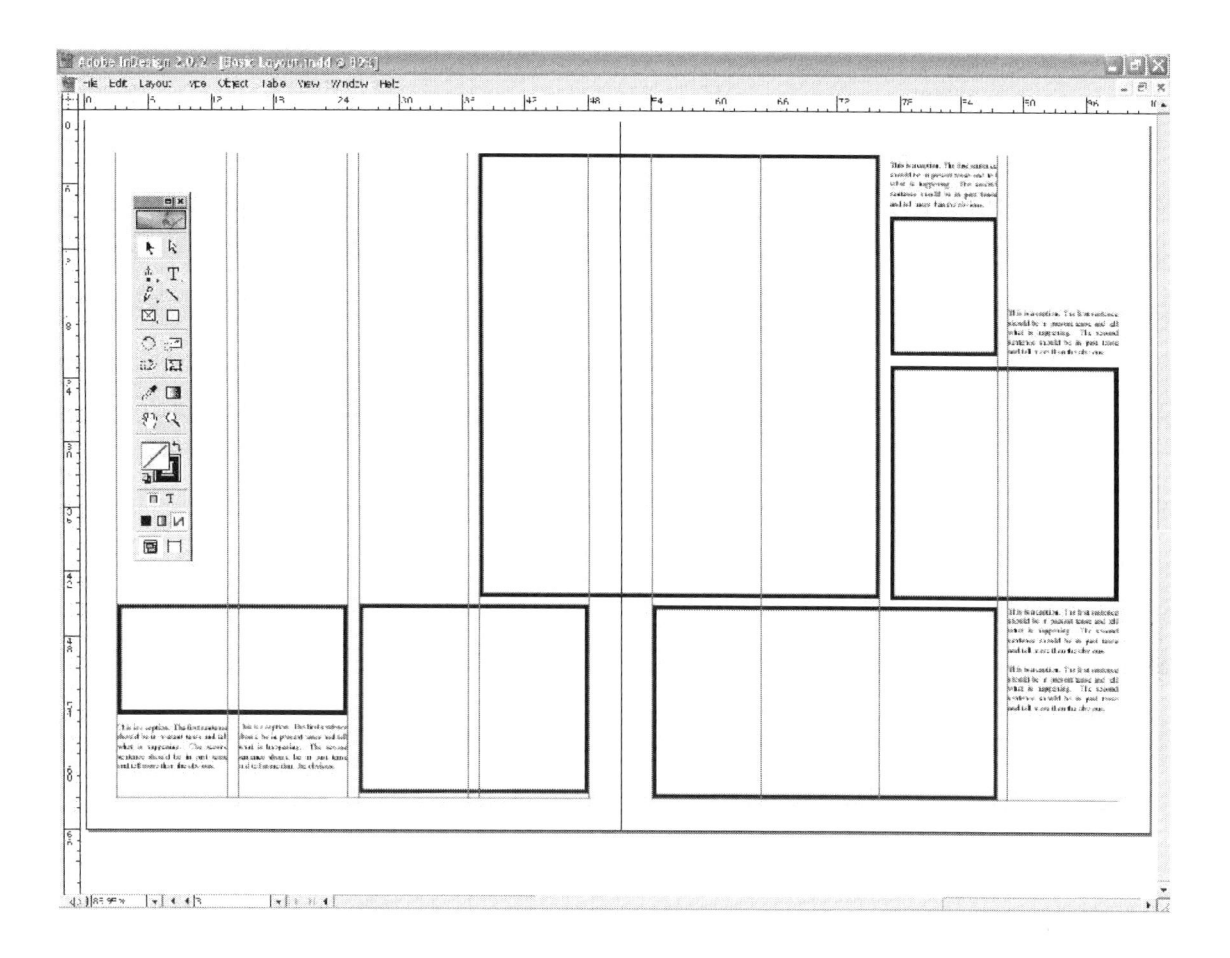

6. Add a headline and body copy. It is okay to have empty (white) space on the corners.

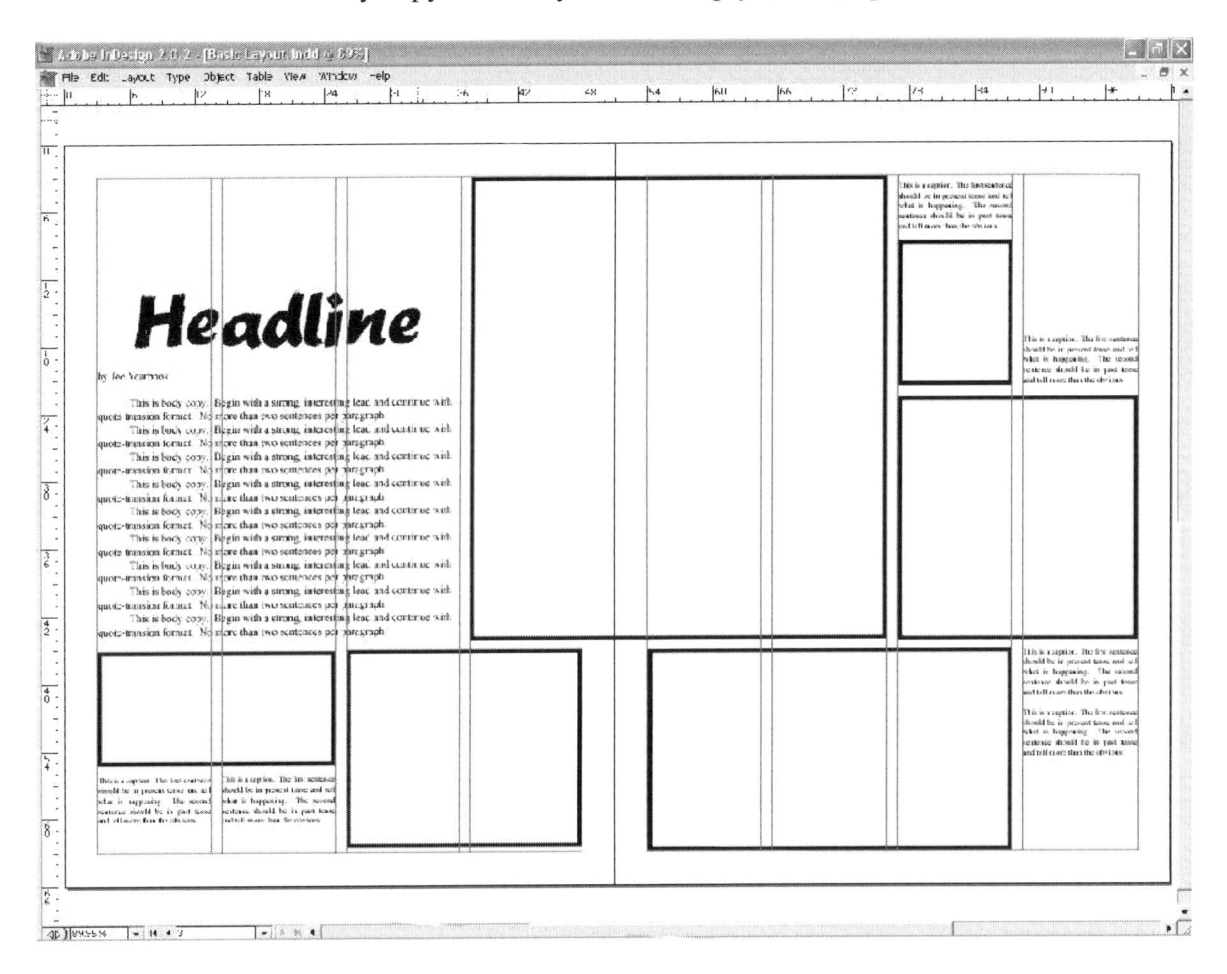

There you have it! A good basic layout!

Advanced Layout

Grid Design

Grid design is very similar to basic layout. It continues to use vertical columns, just more of them.

Ten or twelve columns is not unusual. All the other layout rules are followed. The thing to remember is to always begin and end every element at the edge of a column.

Grid design can get more complicated, integrating varying column widths and horizontal guides as well. Consult one of the sources in the appendix of this guide or your yearbook publisher for advanced design technique.

Modular Design

Modular design is the hottest trend in yearbook design at the moment, along with layout designs that pretty much break all of the rules.

Modular design integrates modules (surveys, charts, quote boxes) into a good basic layout. Staffs can create these modules and keep them on their network for consistency throughout the book. Each module has its own consistent style… font selection, headline style, etc. The designer can then plug in the module that would best show the information he wishes to convey.

Again, this guide is meant to get you started. Consult one of the sources in the appendix of this guide or your yearbook publisher for advanced design technique.

Activity: Create a good basic layout using a four-column format following the basic layout rules.

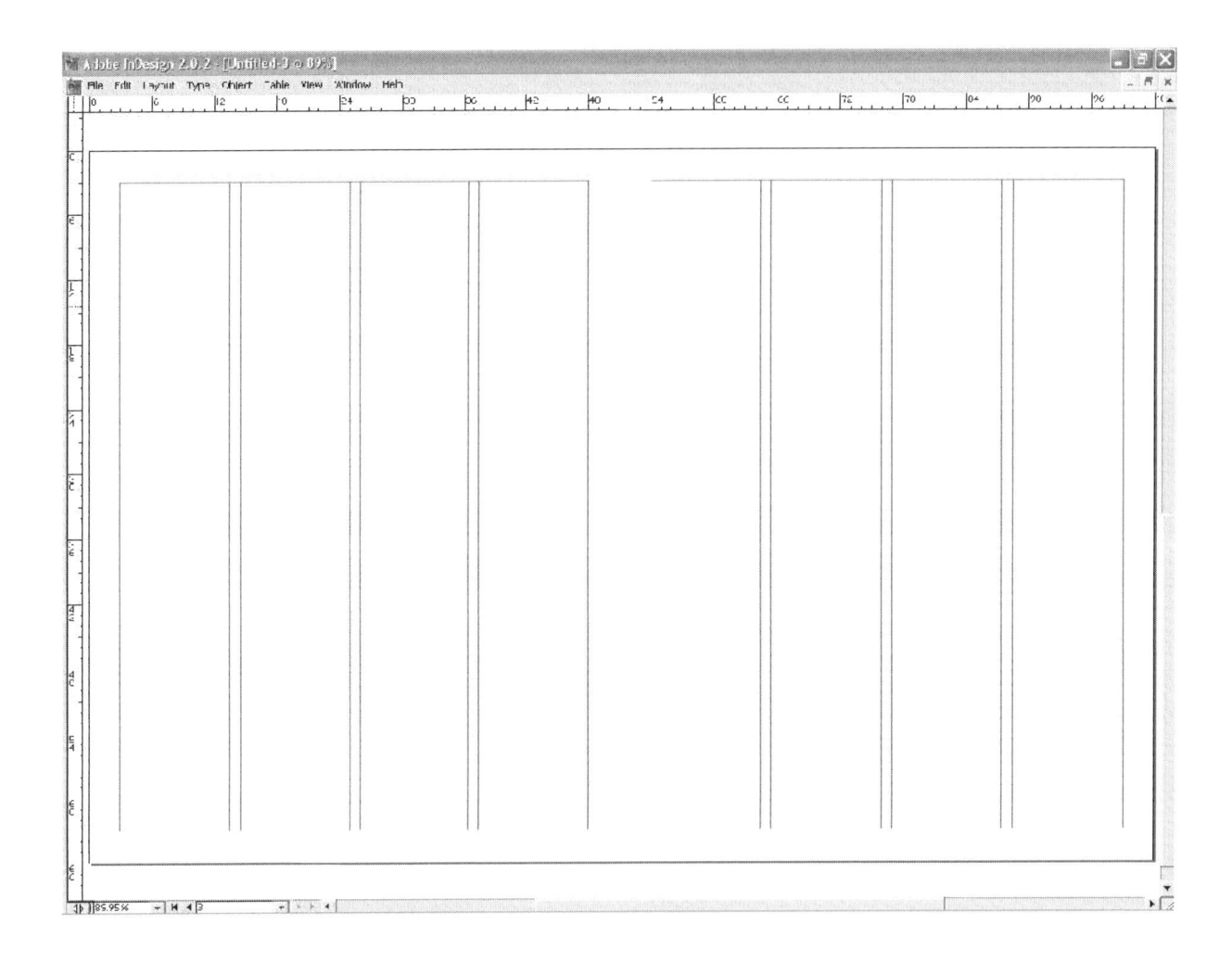

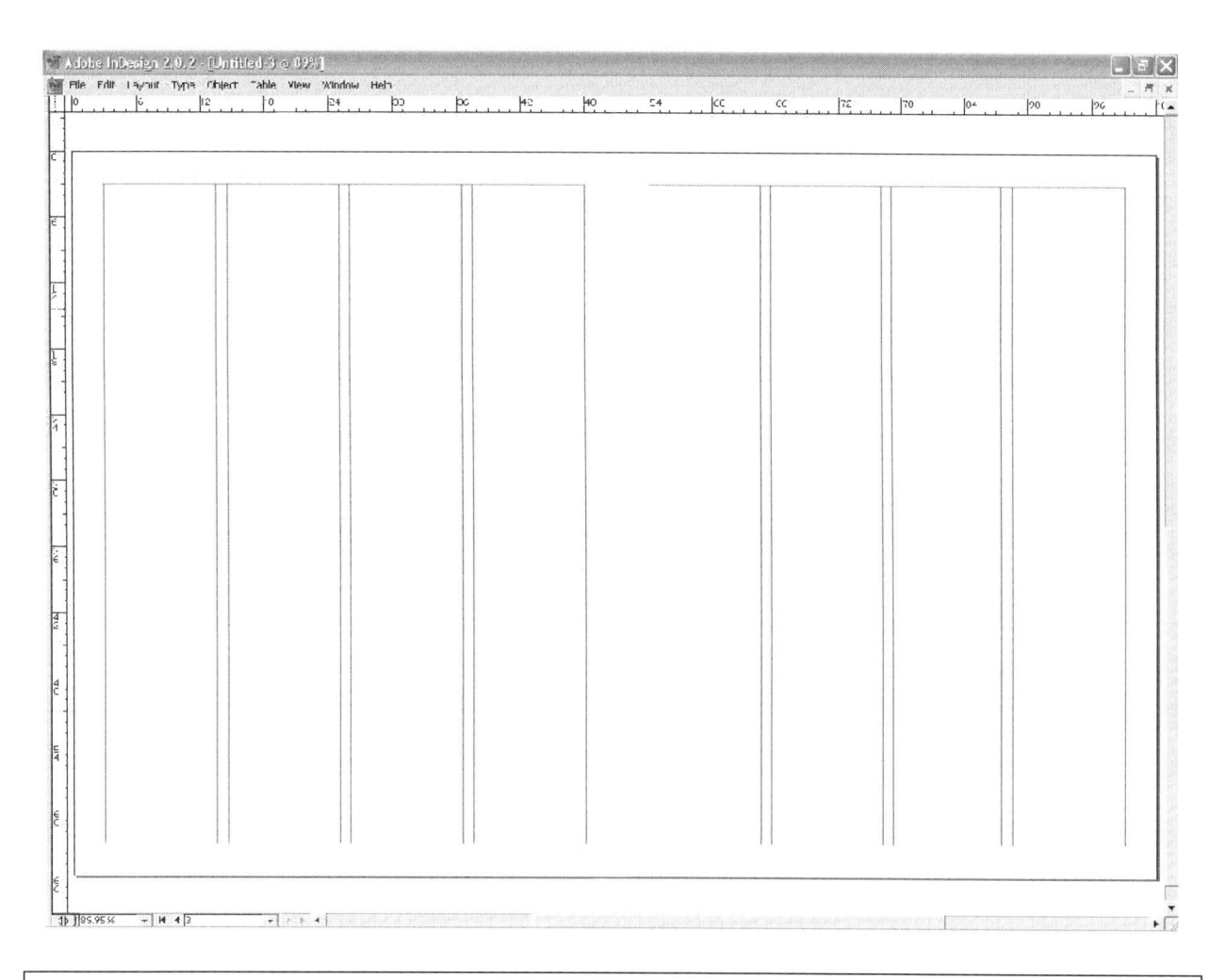

> Activity: Using magazines in the room or that you have brought from home, choose a layout that you like. Be ready to show it and tell what you like about the layout as well as how it follows and breaks "the rules".

Computer Training! Your deadline one team leader will help you get started after an initial demonstration.

How to use the cameras and take good photographs! Your photography editor will teach you individually.

How to sell ads. Your business editor will teach you how to do this in small groups.

Activity: You will create an entire practice layout using InDesign following the instructions on the check sheet. When you have completed this, you will be released to work on deadline One!

Yearbook Adviser Survival Guide

Yearbook Staff Practice Layout Check Sheet
Remember! This deadline is due _____!

TOPIC: How to meet your yearbook deadline.

Work through the process of creating a page. Have each of the following editors approve each part. Editors: You will be held accountable for all quality work you approve.

1. Questions. Write out at least 5 good questions that will get you STORYTELLING QUOTES:

    _____ (Alisha or Alannah)

2. Body Copy. Write your body copy using inverted pyramid style and quote-transition format (At least 5 quotes and transitions). Make sure you have a FANTASTIC lead! Have one of the three editors below check your layout depending on the first letter of your last name.

    _____ (Rachel B A-F, Jenny B G-P, Samantha K R-W)

3. See Kristyn to learn how to use our cameras. Take GOOD pictures of staffers working on deadlines and have her download them.

    _____ (Kristyn M)

4. Make a great basic layout following the rules on page 27 of your handbook. Place your pictures and captions.

    _____ (Rachel B A-F, Jenny B G-P, Samantha K R-W)

5. Captions are in proper format, placed properly (see p.25 of your handbook)

    _____ (Rachel B A-F, Jenny B G-P, Samantha K R-W)

6. Names are indexed properly. Print out an index. Make sure all names are there and that all names are spelled correctly according to the names list.

    _____ (Rachel B A-F, Jenny B G-P, Samantha K R-W)

7. Final check – all elements

    _____ (Jade B)

8. Molter

    _____ (Molter) _____ (Date Completed)

Activity at some point during basic training: Evaluate last year's book and set goals for this year. (An example of what we decided in 208 follows.)

Yearbook Staff 2008:

Keep this stuff in mind...

These are the things the class wanted to either build upon or improve in this yearbook:

PHOTOS
- Keep them interesting
- Define the edges of photos with borders... Make sure they are consistent, though
- No posed pictures

PICKY DETAILS
- Make sure the copy is complete (none cut off)
- byline should look like this (be careful of capitalization... no colon)   by   Kari Molter
- don't rely on the same people in the book... use a variety of people... even ones you don't know!
- PAY CAREFUL ATTENTION TO SPELLING
- PAY CAREFUL ATTENTION TO NAMES
- Make sure the page isn't too "busy"
- Check with the people who have the pages before and after you to make sure you are not all using the same colors.

TEXT / COPY
- Make sure it is in a font and color that is readable
- Make it interesting!
- look at every aspect of what you are writing about
- Use good quotes that make sense! Do the legwork!

COLOR
- consider color in the pictures when choosing colors for your page

TRY THIS FOR A LITTLE CREATIVITY... (just not all the time)
- a headline in an "empty" part of a photo
- pictures inside the letters of a headline
- black and white pictures with a color background
- use a photo with lower transparency and put a headline over the top of it

BASIC TRAINING
(Student Packet)

📖 Yearbook Class Handbook 📖

Staffer: _____

Yearbook Class Handbook

Course Outline
- Introduction, Syllabus
- The Basics of Yearbook Journalism
- Copywriting
- Layout / Computers
- Choose Deadlines
- Production (The rest of the year)

Grading (after basic training)

For each deadline you will have the potential to earn 300 points. Near the beginning of the year, you will have the opportunity to choose the yearbook pages you will be working on. This will result in somewhere between six and eight deadlines.

- ☼ One third of your grade will be determined according to the date your deadline IS ACCEPTED. "Accepted" means that all editors have signed your check sheets and the entire package is accepted by me (Mrs. Molter). More often than not, I will then tell you what you need to fix... you make the corrections, and then get it back to me. YOU WILL NOT EARN A GRADE UNTIL I SAY THAT THE DPS IS ACCEPTABLE.

- ☼ The second third of your grade will be determined by the accuracy of your work. It is incredibly important for us to be accurate when it comes to facts and names. Do you want your name to be spelled wrong in the book? Of course not; every one of the 1200 students in this school feels the same way. For each incorrectly spelled or inaccurate name on your page or in your index, you will lose 10 points from this category. Unsubstantiated quotes (quotes without attached pages from your reporter's notebook signed by the interviewee) will also cause you to lose 10 points per problem. Inaccurate scoreboards will also cause you to lose points. Print out a copy of the scoreboard from the KHS website the day you turn it in to me.

- ☼ The final third of your grade will be determined by your creativity. How interesting is your copy? Your captions? Are your pictures clear and show people's faces? Is your layout interesting, creative, different? Work with your team leader to get comfortable with InDesign so you can do some fun things with your pages.

My best advice to you is to do your work early. If you are having a problem with a deadline, (it is a problem beyond your control) you are to inform me IN WRITING at least ONE MONTH before your deadline date of the problem. Include the page numbers, deadline date, date you are informing me and the nature of the problem. You and I will conference about this problem and come up with an acceptable solution which may (but may not) include an adjusted deadline.

Be aware that people take forever to return information sheets. I DO NOT recommend this method of gathering information from anyone on any subject. Interview people. Talk to them. Don't be shy. Listen for an interesting story. You can't get that from a sheet of questions.
Sports pages take time, probably more time than any other page. Coaches are notoriously UNhelpful. You MUST begin early trying to get information from them. Listen to the announcements and gather information from that. They are posted in the office window. Read them. Also, it will be incredibly difficult to get meaningful quotes concerning any events months after the event has occurred (for example, trying to get quotes about football season in February when you are actually working on that page).

I will be very unforgiving when it comes to late deadlines. You MUST plan ahead and let me know of a problem early. Having done this for nearly 20 years, I know that there are very few legitimate excuses.

If you feel that you do have a legitimate excuse, however, you must submit a letter to me (Yes, IN WRITING) when giving me your final page packet explaining why your work is late and why it was beyond your control. Just so you know, the following excuses are unacceptable: I was absent, I had to work so I couldn't get the pictures, we had a snow day, I had to wait for the editor to check my work, I asked Stacy (or Kim or Mrs. Molter) to take my pictures and they didn't do it or they did a terrible job. GET YOUR WORK DONE EARLY! COME TO VIP, STAY AFTER SCHOOL... GIVE YOURSELF HOMEWORK!

The grading scale is as follows:
- Acceptance **before** your deadline date: "A" with exam exemption credit (100 pts)
- Acceptance on your deadline date: "A" with no exam exemption credit (100)
- Acceptance one day late: "A-"   (92)
- Acceptance two days late: "B+"   (89)
- Acceptance three days late: "B"   (86)
- Acceptance four days late: "B-"   (82)
- Acceptance five days late: "C+"   (79)
- After FIVE days, your DPS will be given to your section editor, and you will earn an "E" in all areas   (0)

Other details about your grade...

1. The first quarter may also include quizzes or assignments on yearbook skills and/or a project.
2. I reserve the right to adjust your grade or revoke exam exemption at any time if I feel that your classroom behavior warrants this action.
3. First quarter, you will be selling advertisements and promoting the marketing of the book will be a part of your grade. It will count as much as a deadline grade. Your goal will be $300. If you earn $400 you will receive a free yearbook, and for every $50 above that, you will earn a certificate for an extra day on a deadline. There may be other fundraisers as well. You will be expected to contribute to this aspect of our business.

Editors

Your editors have all spent at least one year on the staff already. They know what they are doing. Let them help you. If, at any time, you are not treated with respect by any editor, you are expected to let your adviser know. They are, however, responsible for keeping you on track for meeting your deadlines, so accept their help, ask for it, and do your best. They are responsible for letting your adviser know how you are doing, so they are not being nosy, they are trying to help us all meet our deadlines.

Semester Grades

Semester grades will be determined using a point system. Each deadline will be worth 300 points. The first quarter grade will be counted as a percentage and will be worth 40% of the final grade, the second quarter grade will be counted as a percentage and will be worth 40% of the final grade, and the exam will be counted as a percentage and will be worth 20% of the final grade.

Exam Exemption

As a reward for completing your work early, you can be granted exemption from your mid-term and final exams. It is very important that you keep this page and have it signed when you earn exemption from your exam. My records will not be able to tell if you have earned exemption, so please keep close track of this page.

Deadline 1   Due: _____   Completed: _____   Teacher Signature: _____

Deadline 2   Due: _____   Completed: _____   Teacher Signature: _____

Deadline 3   Due: _____   Completed: _____   Teacher Signature: _____

Deadline 4   Due: _____   Completed: _____   Teacher Signature: _____

Deadline 5   Due: _____   Completed: _____   Teacher Signature: _____

Deadline 6   Due: _____   Completed: _____   Teacher Signature: _____

Deadline 7   Due: _____   Completed: _____   Teacher Signature: _____

Deadlines

Record your deadlines here. Be absolutely accurate.

Deadline	Date Due	Page No's	Subject	Special Instructions
1				
2				
3				
4				
5				
6				
7				

Schedule

Below is the schedule we will follow as you are taught the basics of copywriting, layout, and computers. I will move quickly, but I will not allow you to go into production until I feel you have mastered this information.

You must master a significant amount of information before moving on to production. The more closely you study the material, take part in our discussion, and work through the assignments, the quicker the lessons will be done and you will have the skills necessary to produce a quality publication.

YOU MUST COMPLETE YOUR PRACTICE ASSIGNMENT BEFORE YOU CAN MOVE INTO PRODUCTION.

THE BASICS OF YEARBOOK JOURNALISM

Pay attention to the demonstrations and lectures. Grab a yearbook from the shelf for today's lecture. Take notes here, making sure to define important terms in a way that makes sense to you (you might want to draw a picture).

- A yearbook is a cross between a _____ and a _____.

- The four functions of a yearbook are:

    - Memory Book:

    - Reference Book:

    - Public Relations Tool:

    - History Book:

- Other important terms:

    - Ladder:

- Theme:

- Signature:

- Flat:

- Title Page

- Division Pages:

- Endsheets:

- Opening / Closing Sections:

- Index:

- Colophon:

- Sections of the book / Types of pages:
  - Student Life:

  - Academics / Clubs and Organizations:

  - Sports:

- Mugs:

- Community:

- How important is a theme and where does it get developed in a book?

- Legal Issues. Define the following terms and how they are important to you as a yearbook staffer:

    - First Amendment to the Constitution of the United States:

    - Tinker Ruling:

    - Hazelwood Ruling:

    - Copyright:

    - Libel:

    - Privacy:

    - Obscenity

COPYWRITING

Activity: With a partner, look in some of our old yearbooks and yearbooks from other schools. See how the theme is developed. Find interesting copy... story copy, captions, and headlines. As a group, we will share and discuss what makes the writing good. Be ready to contribute your findings.

Prewriting

Who are our potential readers?

What aspects of students lives should be covered?

Do you ever give YOUR opinion?

Ways to get information for your pages:

Interviewing

Your articles will be created by gathering interesting quotations from students and staff then placing them in your article that gives all the necessary facts in an interesting way. Therefore, interviewing is an extremely important skill to learn.

- **The Interviewing Process:**
    1. Make an appointment
    2. Prepare questions ahead of time
    3. Write down key facts, not every word
    4. Verify direct quotes
    5. Organize notes immediately after the interview
    6. Last question: Do you have anything you want to add?

- The "5 W's and one H" are the basis for any interview and article. Make sure you find out the WHO, WHAT, WHEN WHERE, WHY, and HOW about your topic.
- The better the questions, the better the quotes.

- **Questions to avoid in an interview:**
    - No leading questions (ie. How much did you hate losing out as homecoming queen ?)
    - No "feelings" questions (ie. How did you feel when you were crowned queen?)
    - No yes/no questions (you don't get good quotes that way)

- **You DO want STORYTELLING QUOTES.**
    - Concentrate on the human interest aspect
        - *How did you benefit from your community service work?*
    - Ask questions that will make the person think
        - *What was the most satisfying aspect of being a peer leader?*
        - *What was the most frustrating aspect?*
        - *What would you have done differently?*
        - *Why are you active in this club?*

Writing Body (Story) Copy

General Information

Your body copy must be written in past tense. Why, you ask? It's simple. When the book is delivered in the fall, all of the events have happened already... in the past. Thus, past tense.

Each paragraph will contain no more than two sentences. This is why... our columns are not very wide. Any more than two sentences will make your article difficult to read.

Deliver the 5 W's and 1 H. In twenty years, the details of an event will have been lost. It's your job to preserve them for the whole school. Think back to the four purposes of a yearbook... why you are doing this. It's to preserve the *history* of this year, serving as a *record* of the events, keep the memories, and show the community

Don't just say "said". Check out the pages in this handbook that suggest other ways to say this word. Just make sure you are using an appropriate word. Connotation is important.

Quote-Transition Format and the Cut-Off Test

In the simplest of terms, your body copy must tell the story of an event or a season in an interesting way. It is your job to bring the moments to life so people who read the book in twenty years will feel like they are there again.

Articles are written in **Quote-Transition Format**. This is why you need good, storytelling quotes. This is a simple process, really. Interview people about your page, then choose the best quote, next best quote, next best quote and so on until you get to the worst one. Write your article using your best quote first then the least interesting and/or informative quote at the end. This is important because you may need to cut off the end of your article when you place it onto your page. If your least interesting / informative quotes are at the end of your article, you won't lose any important information or have to totally rewrite your article. An article that is written in this manner will pass the **cut-off test** and make your job easier.

The Lead

You will begin your article with a lead. A lead is brief, creative, and original. It is meant to make your reader want to read the rest of the article. You are trying to catch the reader's attention with your lead. Below are several types of leads you can use. We will discuss the examples and then look for some more in old yearbooks for you to add yourself.

3 or 4 well-chosen words

Gasoline, oil, cookies, perm solution... these are just a few smells students encountered at the Genesee Area Skill Center.

School, sports, after-school jobs, money, and family all seem to stress the average high school student, considering every student has obligations and responsibilities to live up to in and out of school.

Barbie dolls that walk, Nerf guns with extra power, fuzzy stuffed animals that you can teach to talk, all of these things have young adults making stops at their local toy store.

Pogo Voodoo, Big Apple, Food Processor, Shooting Butterfly... is this a new foreign language? (article on hacky-sacks)

_____

_____

_____

A description using sensory details

The sky was dark and pierced by lightening; the rain fell steadily as cheers erupted from the stands and the announcers told jokes. Everything was the same as the average Friday night football game—except it was Monday, and the girls ruled the field.

The television set clicked on and all eyes were focused on the screen. It was the beginning of fifth hour and the announcements were about to begin.

The score was 18-20 with the jayvee hornets down by two; Three seconds were left in the game. All Kearsley needed for a victory against Clio was a field goal.

_____

_____

_____

An unusual or thought-provoking question

Are your friends dependable? Are they there for you when you need them? Well, many friends at KHS are.

Mix together 16 veteran cheerleaders, two new coaches, and a new mascot. Whay do you get?

_____
_____
_____

An interesting quote

" The players had the talent, tradition, and ability to do their best and win," quoted Mr. Mike Smith, and he was absolutely right.

" If I could change anything about myself, it would be my attitude. Sometimes I have a bad attitude towards my family and it really is not nice of me to act like that, because they don't deserve it," stated Kristy O'Brien.

_____
_____
_____

A summary

The Varsity Softball team has been on a ten year winning streak, but unfortunately that all changed this year.
Service learning was a great way for Kearsley students to reach out to the community.

They were exposed to new people and things that may not have been a part of their everyday lives. Many of the students enjoyed the feeling that they got when they made someone smile.

The Kearsley Chess team had an incredible season filled with many highlights and achievements. The Chess team tied for first in the league with Powers in addition to taking first and second in two different State Championship meets.

_____
_____
_____

A teaser

The lights went dim. the audience finished up their last conversation until intermission, and the curtain was lifted. Already standing on the stage were actors Kedree Olds (Mugsy) Randy Houghton (Legs) and Adam Washington (Dan Bartone).

It was Christmas time at Kearsley, and Mr. Jones' third hour political science class was acting as Santa Claus.

Teachers, imagine this: You open your classroom door after the room has been occupied by another class. As you turn on the lights you notice every one of your desks has been turned upside down in the middle of the classroom. Is it a case of desk vandalism? Why no, it's a teacher prank!

_____
_____
_____
_____

A Sample Article (annotated)

Shake and Fake

The lights dimmed and the crowd grew silent. Seconds later, as the stage lit up, (quote)
you would think someone would start singing, but that wasn't the case.

This was the annual Lip Sync Contest and to win, you simply had to fake it. Returning (transition)
three-time champ Brad Gilleland was one of the crowd's favorites.

"I tried to work the crowd the best I could, but obviously that didn't work out too well" (quote)
Gilligan exclaimed. "It's not so much that I placed second, because I'm a good sport; a lot of people came up to me afterwards and told me I should have won, but it's okay… you win some, you lose some.

Even with the reigning champ at hand, some acts prepared heavily for the contest (transition)
while others basically winged it on stage.

"I wasn't prepared at all because I hadn't planned on doing it and I put it together the (quote)
night before" Leah Blakenship confessed.

This year, Gilleland was dethroned by Alex Groban and Brianna Desrochers. Even (transition)
with the winning act, Groban said they had a rough time choosing a song to perform.

"We were going to do "What I've Been Looking For" then Brianna called me and said (quote)
that she had a dream and she wanted to do "My Humps" Groban explained. "Then we decided to not do that song s we chose "Breaking Free" because we knew that one would be a crowd pleaser."

(There is more to this article, but you get the idea, right? Quote, transiton, quote, transition, quote, transition.)

Concluding your article

- Do not write a conclusion. Just end your article with a quotation and be done with it. Why? Remember the cut-off test? You might have to cut off the end of your article to make it fit into the space you have available. Another reason to NOT write a conclusion is that you have a limited amount of space in which to present your event. Use that space to show what happened.
- Do not write about the future as you conclude your article. Talk about what happened this year, not what might happen in the future.
- Another temptation to resist is praising the team. (Great season, guys!) That's giving your opinion and it must be avoided.

Headlines

- All good headlines are specific, positive, and free of editorializing.
- They tell the reader something important, don't just serve as a label
- Write them in past tense.
- They present a complete thought in descriptive nouns and strong verbs. Use adjectives sparingly.
- They don't rehash the article's lead.
- They don't state the obvious (such as the school's name, mascot, year, or group name)
- Don't use words such as "students" or "seniors"
- Do not use the words "a", "an", or "the"
- Instead of the word "and" use a comma
- Use single, not double quotes

- Avoid copying song or movie titles
- Subheads expand on the headline, give more information. They might appear above or below a headline.
- Some examples of good headlines (we'll go through old yearbooks to find more):

Stir or Snooze
Personal choices and academic pressures dictate the schedules of early risers and late sleepers.

Pulling Through
Tough mental attitude carries swimmers through season to fifth place at state

Trendy Toys
Rollerblades, Koosh balls, and *Assassin* replace hackey sacks and *Pictionary*.

Captions

- Must provide the answers to questions readers will have about the photo (who, what, when, where, and especially the why and how.)
- Each caption must be at least two sentences long.
  - First sentence: present tense, what is happening in the photo
  - Second sentence: past tense, tell additional information… more than the obvious.
- Captions must tell more than the obvious. What happened before and after the picture was snapped? (Hint: take your own pictures and take notes when you take
- them… 5 W's and 1 H plus what happened before and after… what was the outcome of the game… did the guy hit a home run or strike out?)
- All people in the photos must be identified with first and last names.
- In group shots, use the following format:
- Back row: Sally Jones, Joe Forman, and Ron Mantle. Front row: Bill Card, Jim Smith. (Always begin in the back. There is no need to indicate left to right.)
- Teachers should be referred to in this format: Mrs. Kari Molter
- <u>Do not</u> indicate the graduation year of the students (ie. Sophomore Jimmy Neutron)
- Some examples of good and bad captions (we'll search out more in old yearbooks, too.)

- Good and bad: **Mr. Walth presses the new discipline plan into Eric Hule's mind. Mr. Walworth left a lasting impression on many students this year.** (Echo 2000, p.7) (Good: the picture had Mr. Walworth standing with one foot on Eric while talking into his walkie-talkie. The word "presses" in the first sentence is good, it fits with the picture, and the student's full name is there. The first sentence fits with the theme of the page, the new discipline system. Bad: the second sentence is a filler. It tells nothing new, adds no important information to the caption.)

- Good: **Inspired by the music groups ICP and Twiztid, Brett Ayer shows off his bright red hair. Later in the year, Ayers was seen showing off his hair in a bright blue color.** (Echo 2000, p.9) (The first sentence is in present tense and names the student in the photo as well as gives interesting information… why he colored his hair. The second sentence, in past tense, gives more information, tells more than the obvious.)

- Terrible: **Captain Melissa Pake is putting. She was practicing for a match.** (Echo 2000, p.177). (This is a totally obvious caption. You guessed it, the girl in the picture is putting. The writer needed to do more research here. She could have interviewed the girl and gotten a quote for this caption to add more information than just the obvious. She could have done more research and found out how the girl contributed to the team. Another thing the person creating the page could have done is get to the matches and take better pictures instead of just settling for posed shots.)

- Excellent: **The Owosso defense looks on with astonishment as Emily Androswky heads in the tying goal in the district semifinals. Emily had three goals and five assists throughout the season.** (Echo 2000, p.179). (This is one of those captions that is helped because the picture is great. The staffer went to games and made sure to get great pictures. Because of this, she was able to capture an important moment in an important game. The first sentence is good because it identifies the team we were playing against and the center of attention in the photo... Emily Androwski. The photo tells why this was an important moment. The second sentence adds important information about this player.)

- Terrible: **With Joseph Veneguhs we thought we were in Vegas. He was the ace up our sleeve.** (Echo 1996 p.14). (It's a football page. The caption starts its first sentence with a stupid rhyme which gives little information about what he is doing, who he's playing against, etc. It is in past tense, which is also a problem. The second sentence tells nothing. It's pure filler.)

Layout

Good Photographs

- Capture the action and reaction, expression and emotion of a moment.
- They reach out to readers and tell stories that captions, headline and body copy complete.
- Have a story to tell.
- Capture a reader's attention.
- Are clear, not blurry
- ZOOM WITH YOUR FEET! GET CLOSE TO THE ACTION!
- Cover from all angles.
- Think UNIQUE and EXCITING!
- Check out some good and bad examples from yearbooks…

Layout

Before you can even begin to create the layout for a page, there are some terms you must get used to.

- Dominant photo: The largest photo on the page. It gets the attention of the person right away when he or she looks at the page.
- Two-page spread (DPS): Double Page Spread. We look at the facing pages of a spread as one thing, not two separate pages.

- External Margins: White space on the outside of a page.

- Internal Margins: The distance between elements on a page.

- Columns: Many good basic layouts use a column format. We will practice this.

- Eyeline: An internal margin that goes across both pages to draw the reader's eye across the page.

- Rule Lines: Lines around pictures or lines on a page for a design purpose.

- Screens: blocks of color or grey on a page.

Basic Layout Rules

1. Start with a dominant photo that is at least 2 ½ times larger than any other photo on the spread. Place it toward the center of the page.

2. Other Pics: 3-7 per page (try to make different shaped photo boxes, some long, some tall, some square), place them toward the center of the page.

3. One grid internal margins, create an eyeline.

4. Captions: stack no more than 2. Place them on the corners of your layout. They must touch the picture to which they belong.

Basic Layout

Column Format

This is the most basic type of layout. Once you have some time to practice this, then you can expand to more complicated types of layout such as grid design and modular design.

Keep in mind that this is very basic layout. Color, photo choice, and font choice are not addressed here. A good exercise is to pick apart appealing layouts from other yearbooks and, later, magazines, to analyze their layout technique.

1. Begin with a double page spread (two facing pages).

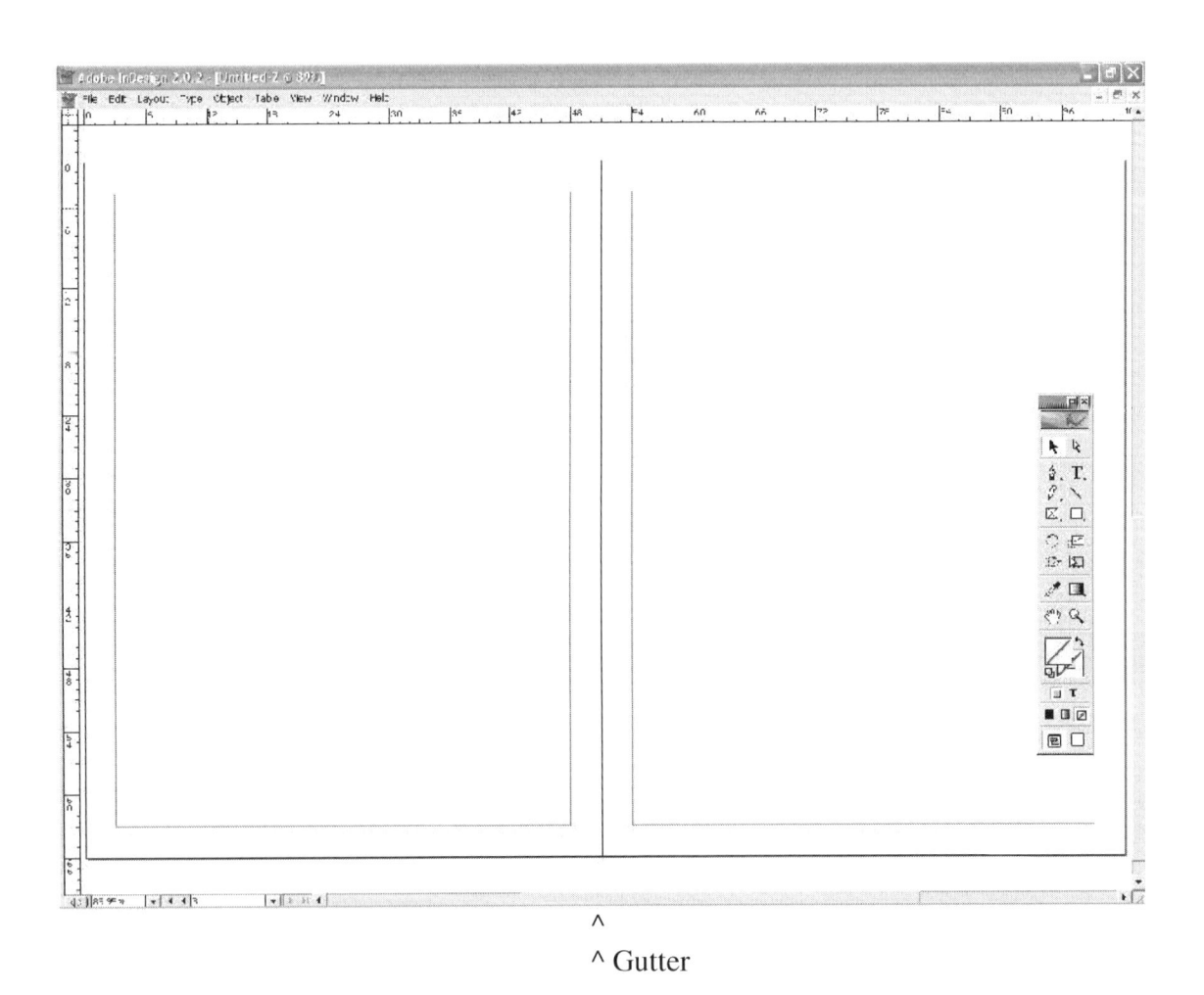

^ Gutter

2. Chose the number of Columns You wish to use. Typical column formats are three, four, and five. The following example is a four-column format… four columns on each side. The key is always stopping and starting on a column line.

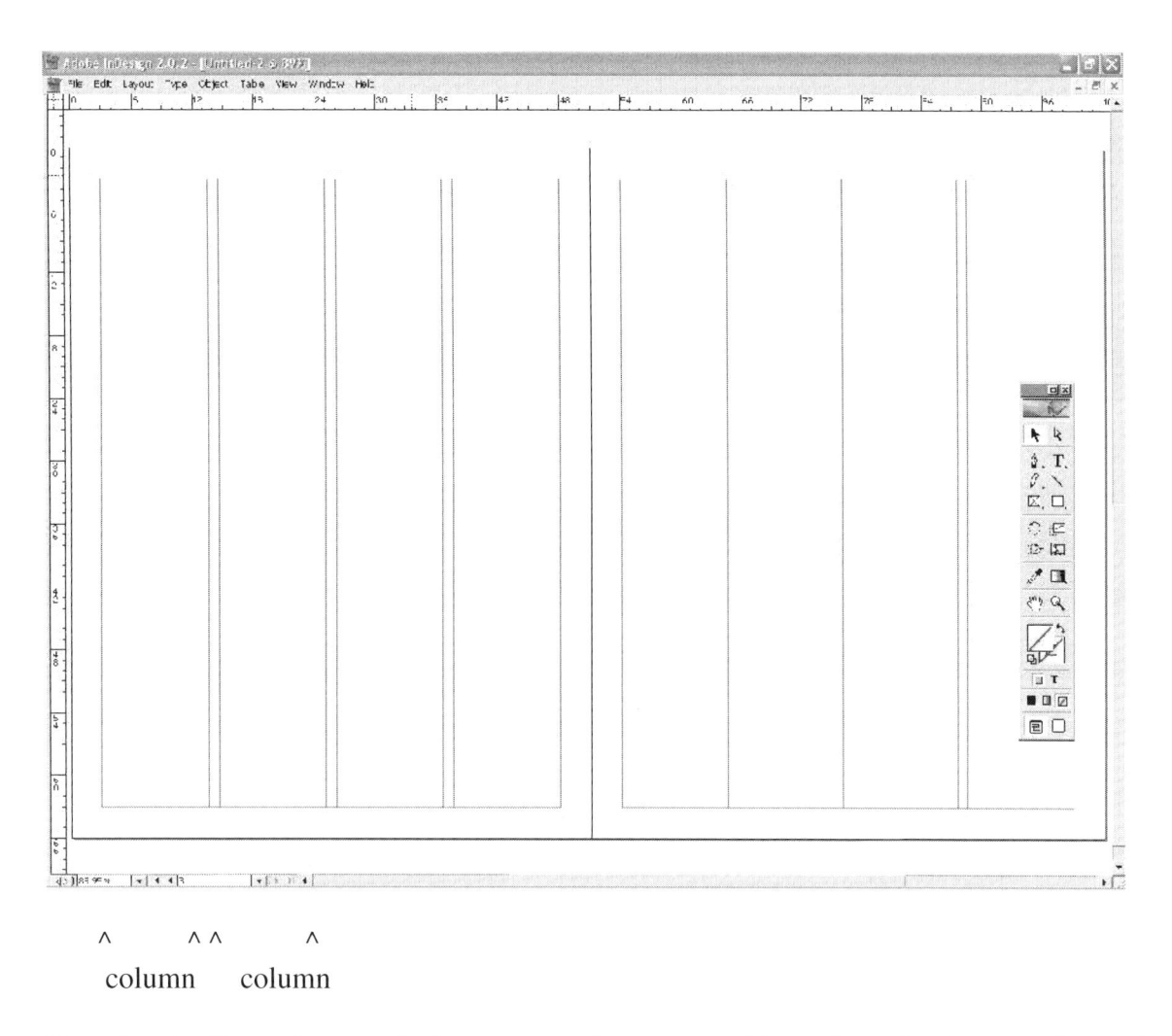

˄   ˄ ˄   ˄
column   column

Note that the first column ends then a new column starts. Note where the photos and copy begin and end on the following examples as the layout develops. They always end at the edge of a column. Photos and copy can be more than one column wide, but they always begin and end on a column line.

3. Place a dominant photo near the center of the layout, crossing the gutter to tie the two halves of the page together.

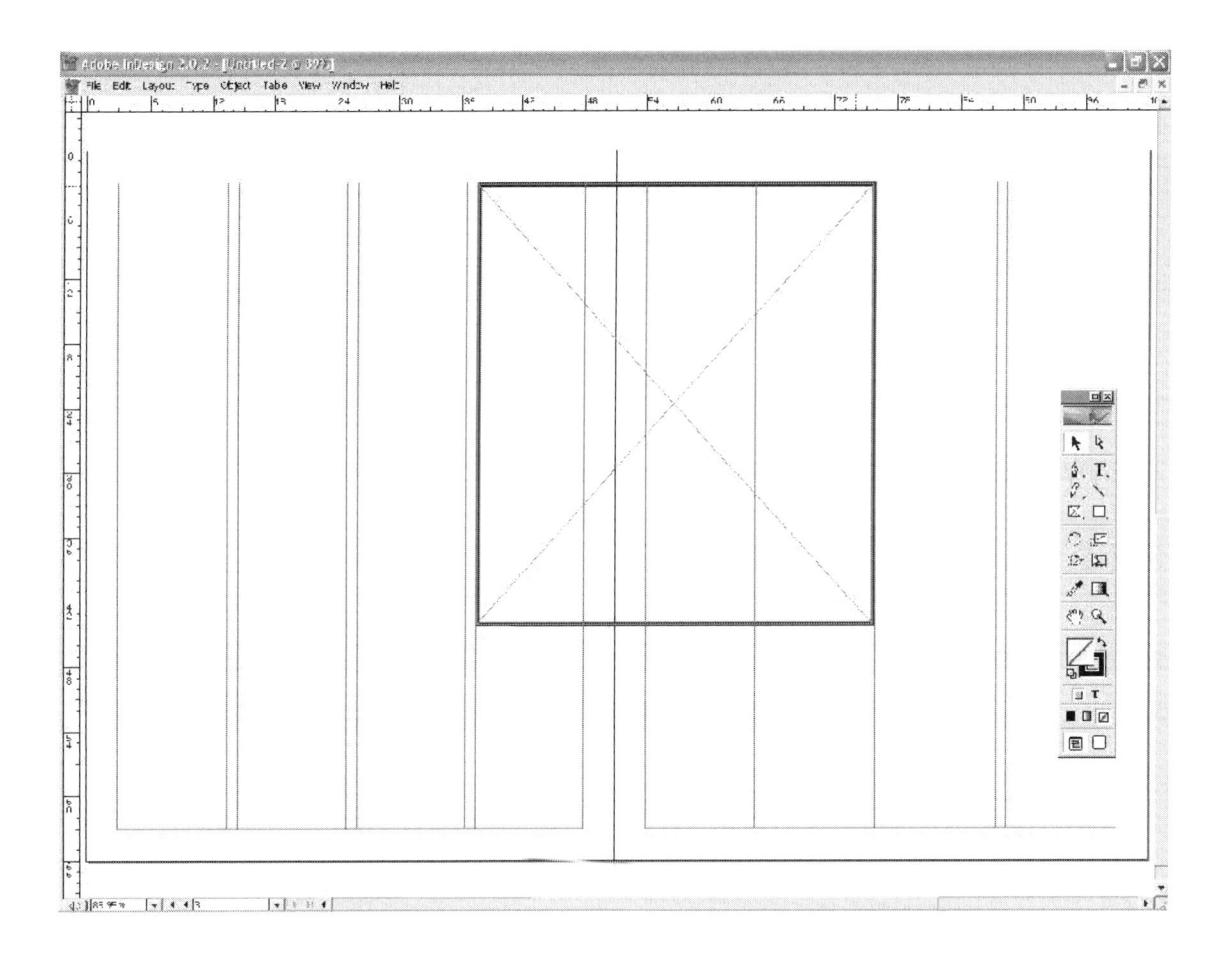

4. Place other photos around the dominant photo… create an eye line. (In this case, the eye line will be below this photo. Use consistent internal margins (space between all photos) and leave room for a headline and body copy as well as captions (which go best on the corners). Use a variety of picture shapes.

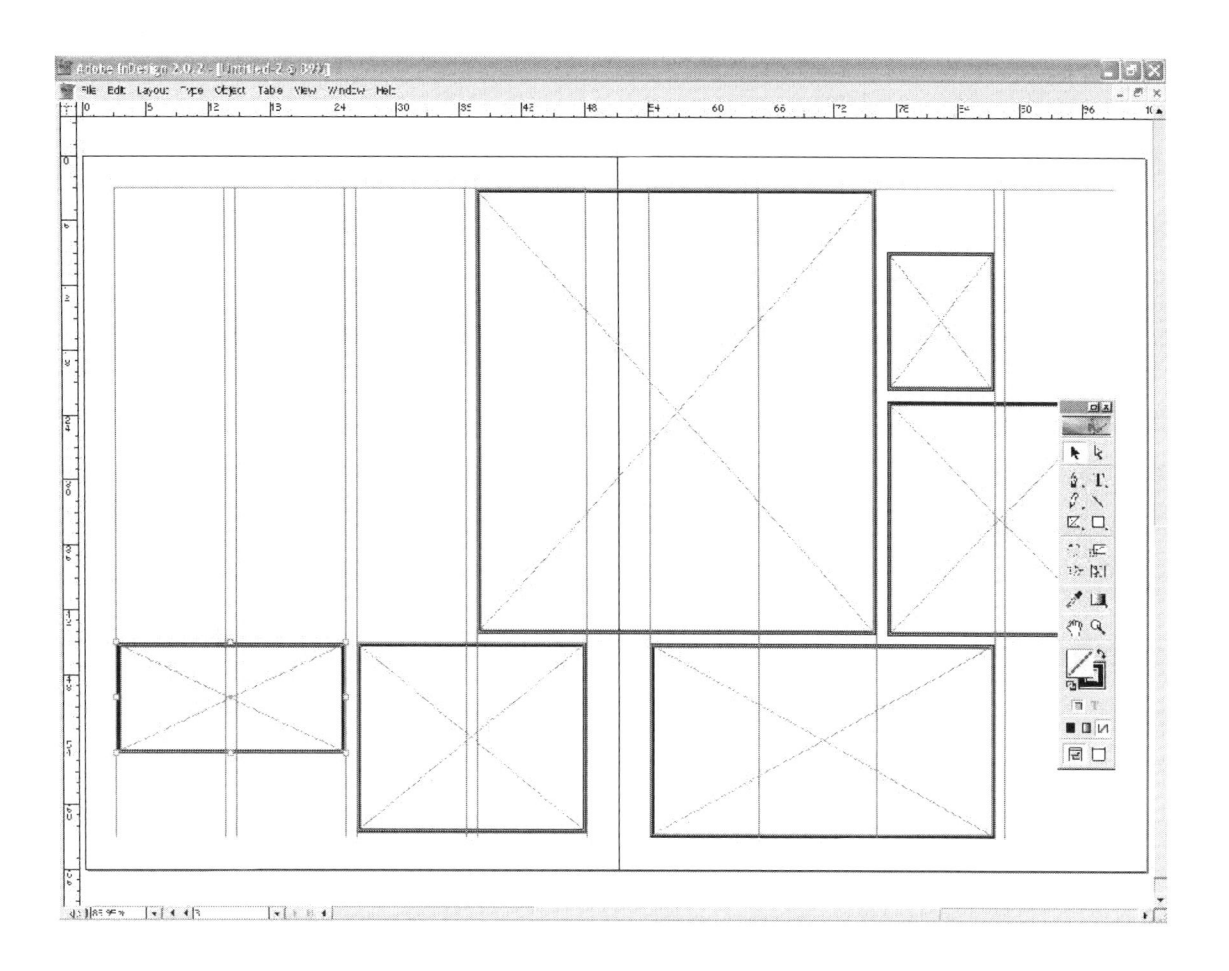

5. Place captions on your layout so they touch the photo to which they belong. Stack no more than two captions. Keep consistent internal margins.

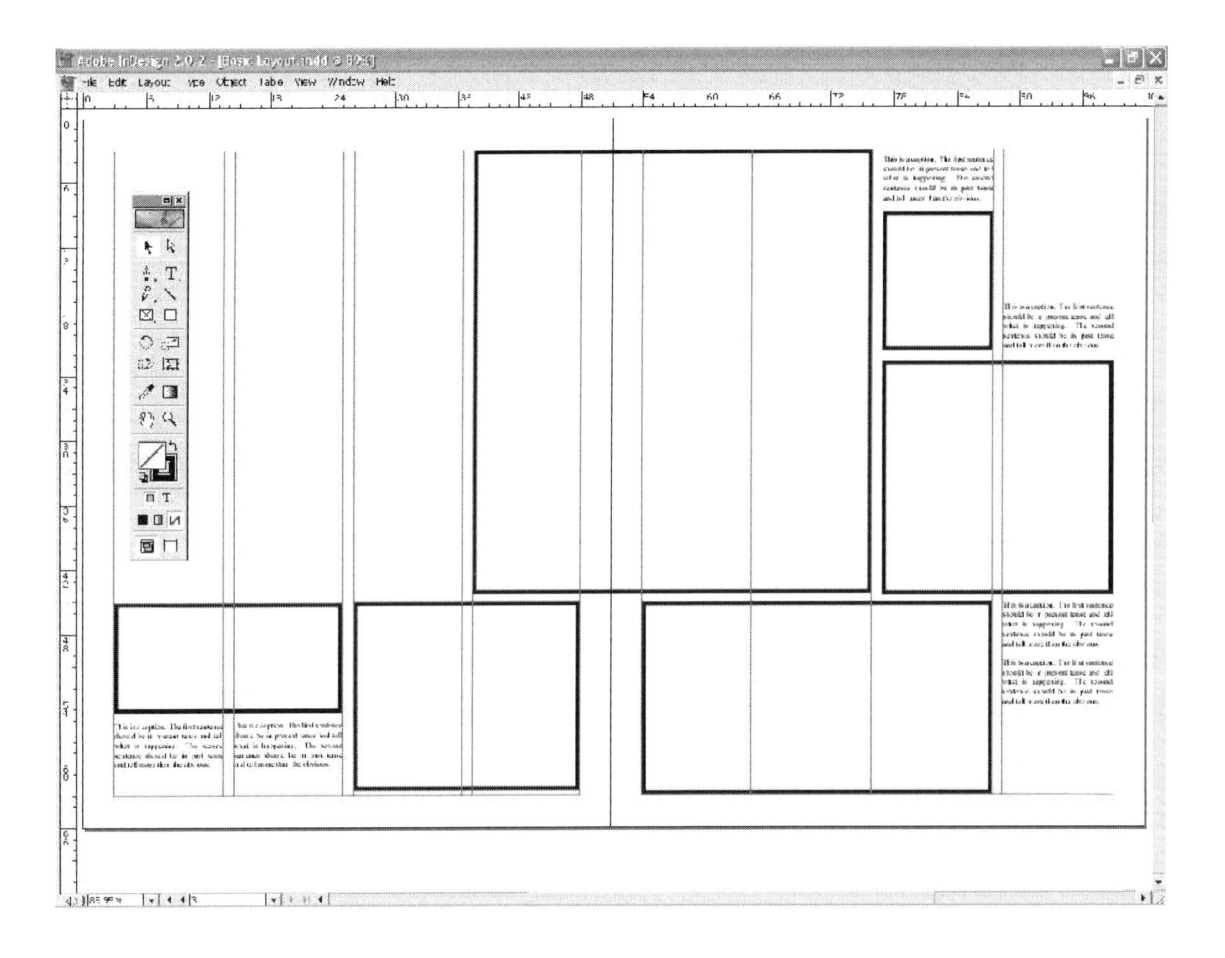

6. Add a headline and body copy. It is okay to have empty (white) space on the corners.

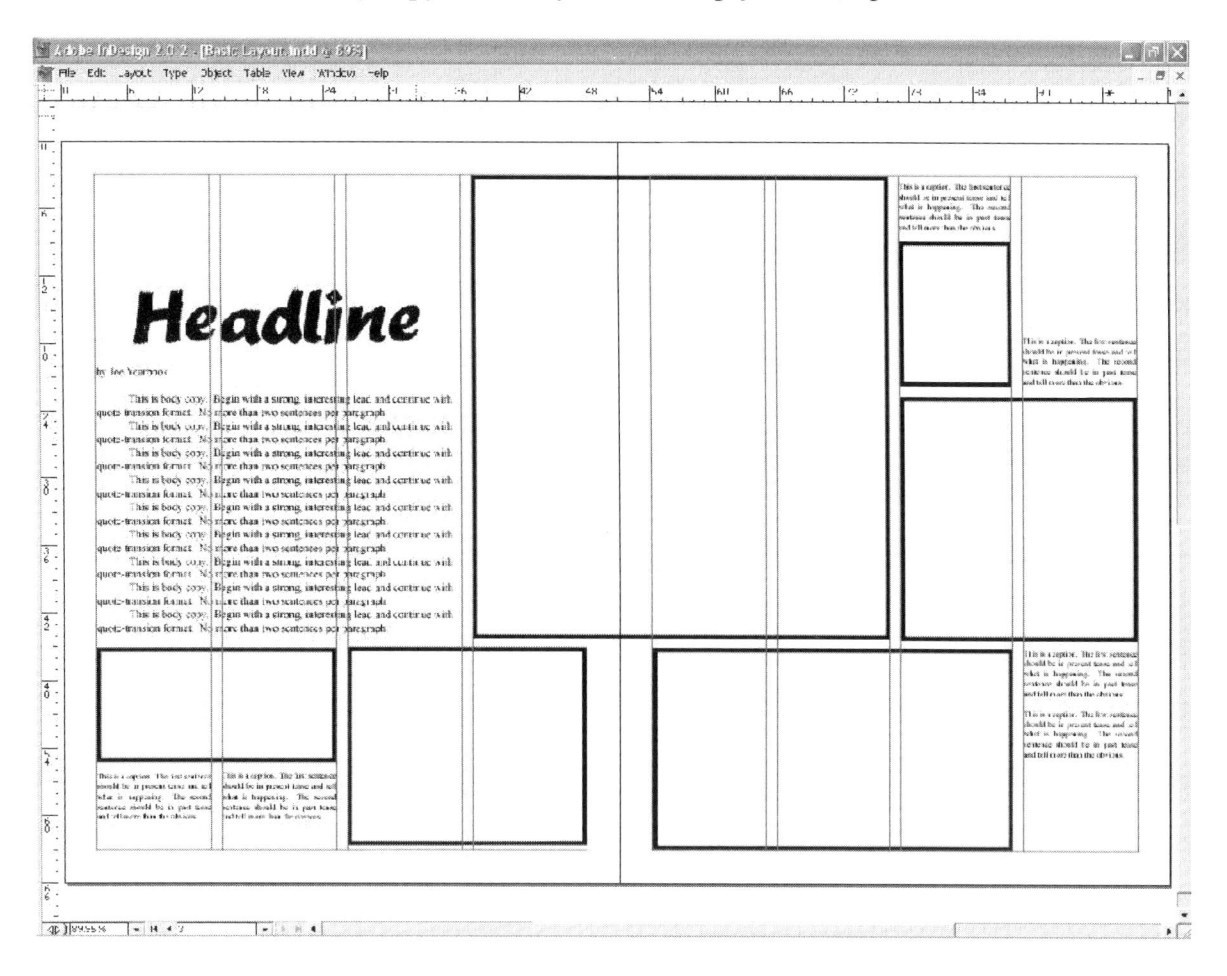

There you have it! A good basic layout!

Activity: Create a good basic layout using a four-column format following the basic layout rules.

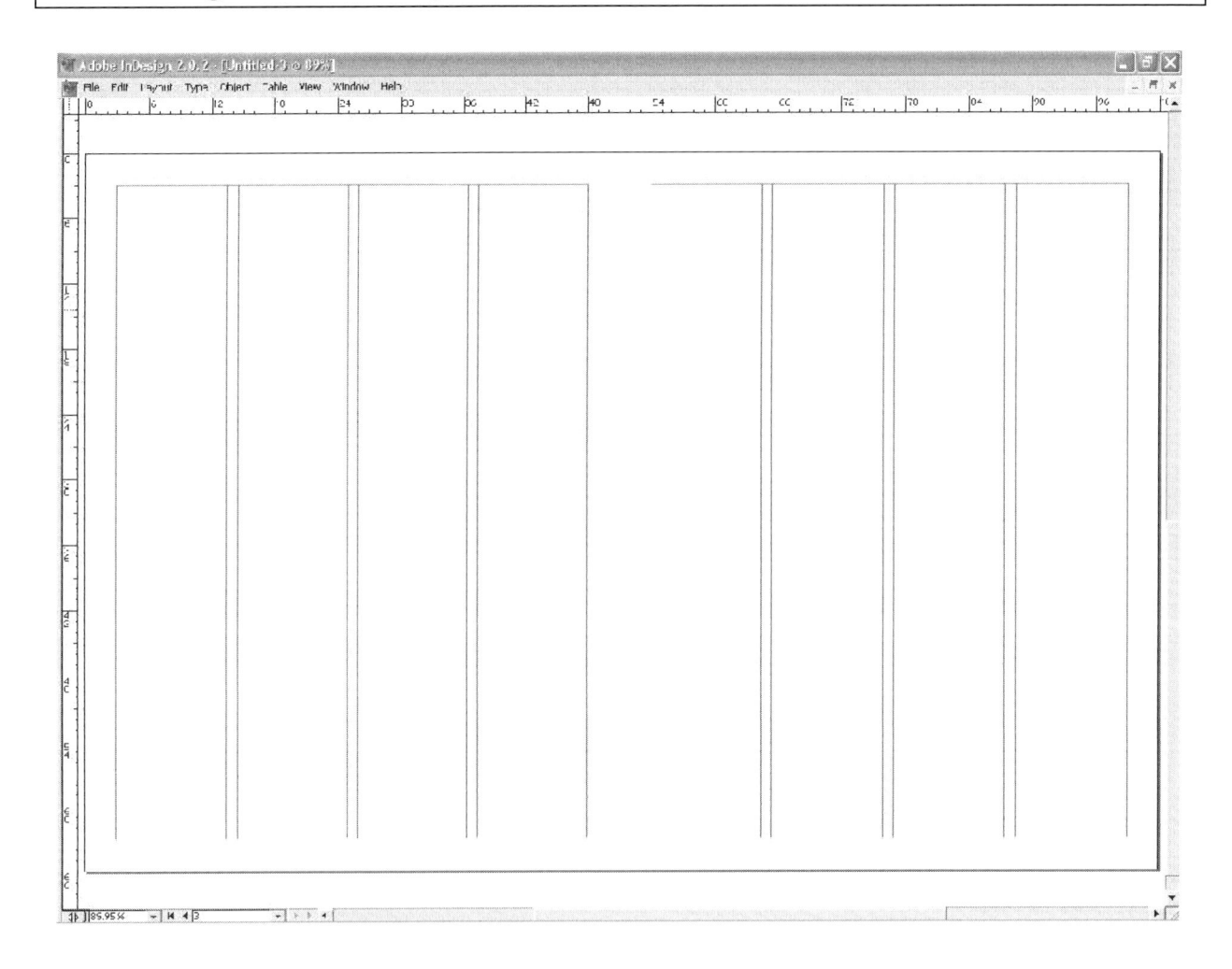

Yearbook Adviser Survival Guide

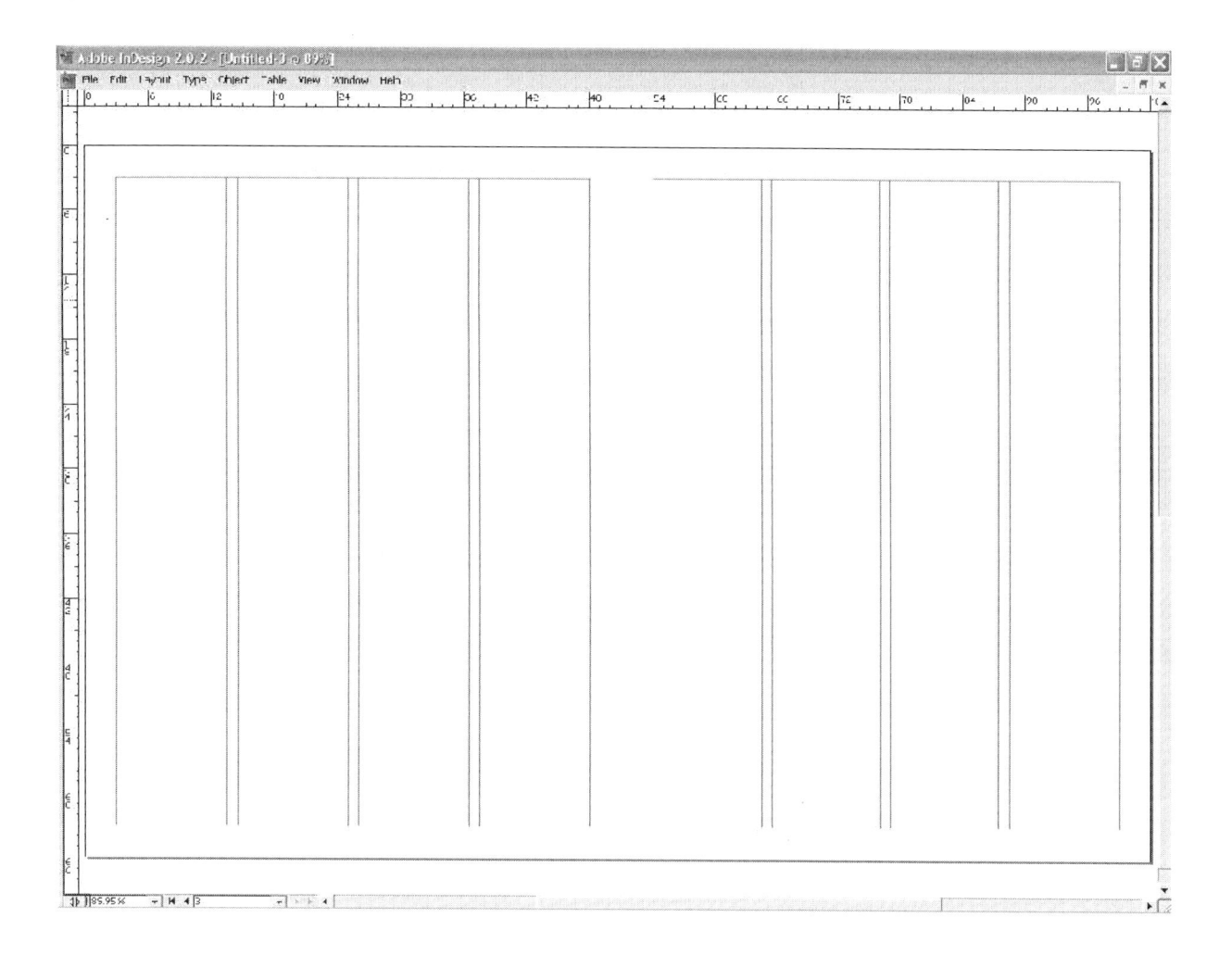

> Activity: Using magazines in the room or that you have brought from home, choose a layout that you like. Be ready to show it and tell what you like about the layout. Consider the following categories: layout, copy, color, headline style.

Computer Training! Your deadline one team leader will help you get started after an initial demonstration.

How to use the cameras and take good photographs! Your photography editor will teach you individually.

How to sell ads. Your business editor will teach you how to do this in small groups.

> Activity: You will create an entire practice layout using InDesign following the instructions on the check sheet. When you have completed this, you will be released to work on deadline One!

Yearbook Adviser Survival Guide

Staff Practice Layout Check Sheet
Remember! This deadline is due _____!

TOPIC: How to meet your yearbook deadline.

Work through the process of creating a page. Have each of the following editors approve each part. Editors: You will be held accountable for all quality work you approve.

1. Questions. Write out at least 5 good questions that will get you STORYTELLING QUOTES:

_____ (Alisha or Alannah)

2. Body Copy. Write your body copy using inverted pyramid style and quote-transition format (At least 5 quotes and transitions). Make sure you have a FANTASTIC lead! Have one of the three editors below check your layout depending on the first letter of your last name.

_____ (Rachel B A-F, Jenny B G-P, Samantha K R-W)

3. See Kristyn to learn how to use our cameras. Take GOOD pictures of staffers working on deadlines and have her download them.

_____ (Kristyn M)

4. Make a great basic layout following the rules on page 27 of your handbook. Place your pictures and captions.
_____ (Rachel B A-F, Jenny B G-P, Samantha K R-W)

5. Captions are in proper format, placed properly (see p.25 of your handbook)

_____ (Rachel B A-F, Jenny B G-P, Samantha K R-W)

6. Names are indexed properly. Print out an index. Make sure all names are there and that all names are spelled correctly according to the names list.

_____ (Rachel B A-F, Jenny B G-P, Samantha K R-W)

7. Final check – all elements

_____ (Jade B)

8. Molter

_____ (Molter) _____ (Date Completed)

Notes:

OTHER POTENTIALLY USEFUL STUFF

YEARBOOK SIGN-OUT SHEET
SIGN OUT AND IN WHEN YOU MUST LEAVE THE ROOM!

Staffer	Date	Where/Why?	Time Out	Time In

Yearbook Adviser Survival Guide

Interim Report: Team Leaders

Team Leader: _____ Date _____

Page Numbers	Staffer	What is completed	Still to be done:

Yearbook Adviser Survival Guide

I'm having a problem with this deadline...

This must be presented to Mrs. Molter NO LATER THAN one month before this deadline is due in order to be considered for a deadline adjustment with no lowering of grade or disqualification for exam exemption credit.

Name _____

Page Numbers _____

Subject: _____

Date DPS is due: _____

Date this notice is submitted: _____

Reason this deadline may be late:

Resolution to the problem (to be written down after conference with Mrs. Molter).

New deadline: ____yes ____no
New deadline date: _____
Student Signature: _____ date _____
Adviser Signature: _____ date _____

Kearsley Echo Stylebook

This brief stylebook is useful because it helps students be consistent. I like to include all of the team names in our conference, and other frequently used words…

A

academic departments: use lowercase, except English

academic titles: capitalize when they are before a name: Principal Karl Paulsen, otherwise, use lower case

adviser, not advisor

assistant principal: use this title for KHS

athletic teams: capitalize teams, associations, and recognized nicknames: the Big Nine, the Raiders

B

Big Nine: the teams are Beecher, Carman-Ainsworth, Clio, Davison, Flushing, Grand Blanc, Kearsley, Powers Catholic, and Swartz Creek

C

cager: nickname for a basketball player

Captains Club (no apostrophe)

Class Day: use caps

Clio: mascot- Mustangs. colors- Orange and Black

cross country: no hyphen

D

Davison: mascot- Cardinals. colors- Maroon and gold

diving: not diveing

E

Eclipse: Our school newspaper. Use The <u>Eclipse</u>

F

freshman, junior, senior, sophomore: lower case unless used before a person's name as a title (ie. Junior Josh Smith or Josh Smith, junior, said that...)

G

grade-point average: also acceptable is GPA

Graduation: capitalize when referring to KHS's ceremony. Otherwise, use lower case.

Grand Blanc: mascot- Bobcats. Colors: red and black

grappler: nickname for a wrestler

gridiron: nickname for a football field

H

Homecoming: capitalize when referring to KHS's

I

injuries: they are suffered or sustained, not recived

J

jayvee: use this form, not JV

junior, senior, freshman, sophomore: lower case unless used before a person's name like a title.

K

K-NEWS (all caps)

L

M

N

nicknames: put quotes around the nickname within the formal name of a person (ie. Paul "Bear" Bryant)

O

official(s): not referee(s)